FREIGHTERS OF MANITOWOC

The Story of Great Lakes Freight Carrying Vessels Built in Manitowoc, Wisconsin

By
Tom Wenstadt

Bloomington, IN 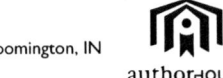 Milton Keynes, UK
authorHOUSE®

AuthorHouse™
1663 Liberty Drive, Suite 200
Bloomington, IN 47403
www.authorhouse.com
Phone: 1-800-839-8640

AuthorHouse™ UK Ltd.
500 Avebury Boulevard
Central Milton Keynes, MK9 2BE
www.authorhouse.co.uk
Phone: 08001974150

© *2007 Tom Wenstadt. All rights reserved.*

No part of this book may be reproduced, stored in a retrieval system, or transmitted by any means without the written permission of the author.

First published by AuthorHouse 5/23/2007

ISBN: 978-1-4259-5838-1 (sc)

Library of Congress Control Number: 2006910574

Printed in the United States of America
Bloomington, Indiana

This book is printed on acid-free paper.

Contents

Preface vii

Acknowledgments ix

Chapter 1 Early Freighters and Other Major Shipbuilding 1847 to 1951   1

Chapter 2 JOHN G. MUNSON   127

Chapter 3 JOHN J. BOLAND III   167

Chapter 4 DETROIT EDISON II   215

Chapter 5 ADAM E. CORNELIUS III   249

Chapter 6 EDWARD L. RYERSON   283

Epilogue 333

Manitowoc Shipbuilder Chronology 335

Bibliography 337

Index 339

PREFACE

As a native of Manitowoc and fascinated with boats from an age earlier than I can remember, interest in the great ships built in my home town was a natural. My father had a photo of the launching of the PETO on his desk where I pondered it for hours. Every time we went downtown, we passed the shipyards on 10th Street. At the time, there was a panoramic view and I caught every glimpse I could as I followed the progress of each vessel as it was being built. Finally it was launch day! I vividly remember telling mom "remember to pick me up to see the launch".

Shipbuilding was a "big deal" in Manitowoc. As far back as the 1850s, large portions of the populous packed the 8th Street Bridge and the surrounding area to watch ships launched. Even the high school athletic teams were - and still are - called the "Ships". Anyone who wanted to attend a launch was willingly excused from school and thousands of spectators turned out. For about an hour before the launch, the pounding of sledge hammers in unison could be heard as hundreds of men pounded wedges between the skid timber bunks and the ship to raise it off the building bunks. Then everything got quiet. Finally, the champagne (likely water) bottle was broken over the bow and the compressed air cutters severed the heavy ropes at each end of the vessel. The huge ship started sliding down the skid timbers and all eyes were glued on it. Then it tipped and crashed into the river with a horrendous splash! Ship and factory whistles blew, the band played and the crowd cheered. The tug boats eased the ship back to the dock through the river that was littered with launch timbers. Over the following months, the vessel was finished off then squeezed through of the narrow twisting river and bridges. Sea trials and a pre-delivery open house were the final send off for each ship.

It was not until I began research for this book that I realized what had happened in the previous 100 years on that same river that led up to these magnificent vessels. This book chronicles the building of freight carrying vessels built in Manitowoc, Wisconsin from beginning to end. Other shipbuilding that was significant in gathering the capability to build the subsequent freighters is also included. The pinnacle of these vessels – and the main focus of the book – are the last five freighters built between 1951 and 1960. Details of each vessel as well as each builder are given in chronological order from the builder's first vessel, and then by the build date of each vessel for each builder. As always, good things come to an end. So great were the accomplishments of the builders of these vessels, that the vessel size outgrew the waterways of Manitowoc and the shipbuilding capability was moved to waterways that could accommodate larger vessels.

As can be observed in the bibliography, ship and builder data was gathered from numerous sources. In some cases not all were in agreement. A significant attempt was made to choose the most authentic and logical information available. After all, this data has slowly dissolved over the last 50 to 150 years.

ACKNOWLEDGMENTS

Chris Wenstadt assisted with research, editing and organization. She was also a patient wife over the years it took to create this book.

The Wisconsin Maritime Museum was most generous and supportive in gathering data for this book. Specifically, I would like to thank Molly Biddle, Cristin Waterbury, Bill Theisen, Norma Bishop, and Robert Peppard.

The Manitowoc Company, Inc. represented by Steve Khail, graciously gave permission to use the numerous construction images.

The Inland Seas Maritime Museum including Christopher Gillcrist, Carrie Sowden, Peggy Bechtol, and Noelle McFarland were very helpful in opening their extensive archives for research.

Suzette Lopez, Mary Malekovicz, and Caroline Caldwell of the Milwaukee Public Library and the Wisconsin Marine Historical Society were another great source of information.

I would like to acknowledge:

Robert Graham of the Historical Collection of the Great Lakes, Bowling Green State University

The Manitowoc County Historical Society Peg Harder, Sarah VanLanduyt and Joan Konecney

Michigan Maritime Museum Coby Ball and Judy Schlaack

Gary Yealon for Manitowoc Shipbuilding images

Doris Burger Hansen for Burger family records

Daryl Cornick for images of the Edward L. Ryerson

Vickie Peasley for records of Jonah Richards

Barbara Nitka and Phil Groll for information on Hans Scove

Charles Peterson for image of his painting of the Burt Barnes

Tim Woodard for computer image assistance

LindyLazar Marketing John Phillips and Karen Soderholm for cover design and proofing

CHAPTER 1

Early Freighters and Other Major Shipbuilding 1847 to 1951

Manitowoc, Wisconsin was a natural for shipbuilding in the late 1840s. With the rapid population growth, there was an unfilled demand for transportation of goods and people, and waters of the Great Lakes were the highway of the day. Manitowoc had a partially navigable river at the head of a wide deep bay on the western shore of Lake Michigan that was protected by a pier and identified by a lighthouse. The river itself was deep enough to float the largest laden vessels of the day, however, there was a sand bar across the river as it entered the lake. Only smaller vessels could cross the bar while midsize ships could cross only by riding larger waves off the lake. Larger vessels could only moore out in the lake. Beginning in 1837, local shipping interests made a succession of governmental attempts to get improvements for the Manitowoc Harbor. With no action as of 1848, a bridge pier was built off the south side of the river by Case and Clark. The lighthouse was built in 1839 and was located at the corner of 5th and York Streets. These improvements, plus was an abundant supply of timber, foundries, and the all important skilled labor force were all in place. These circumstances lead to the shipbuilders you will read about in Chapter 1.

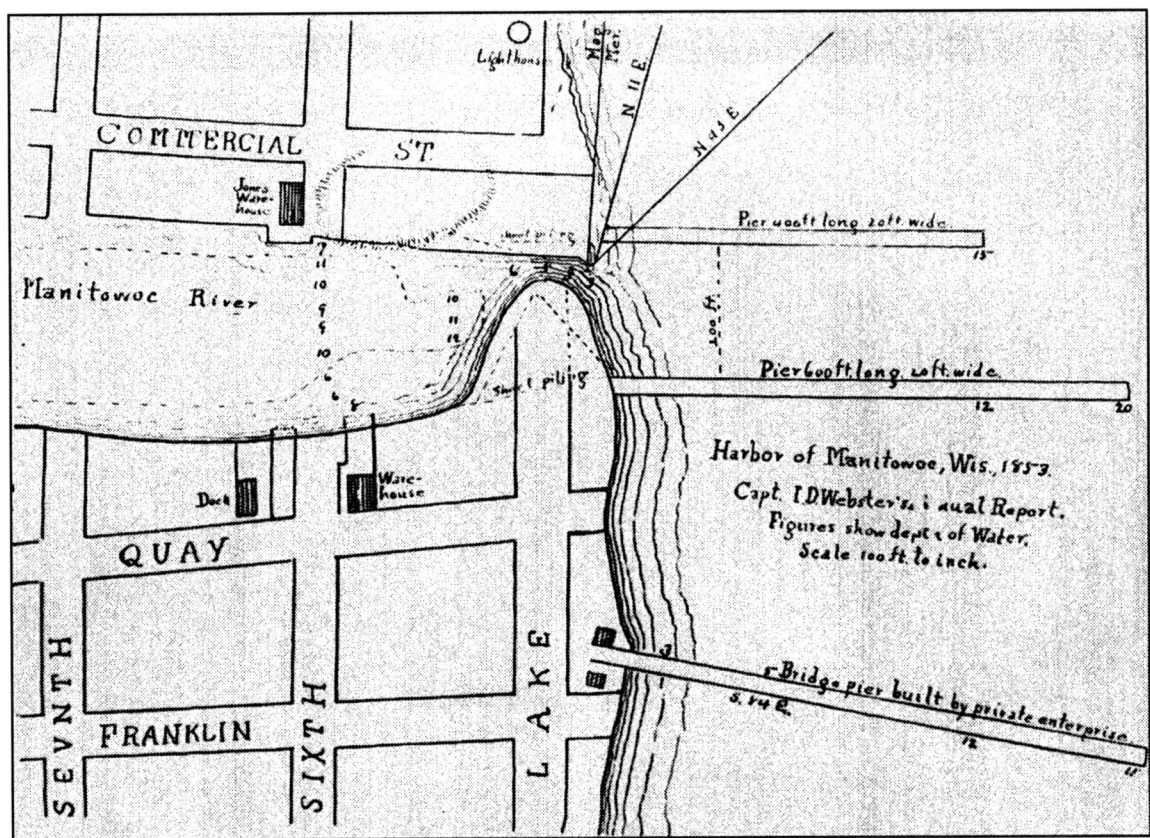

Manitowoc County Historical Society, INC

Sketch of the Manitowoc Harbor, circa 1853

Captain Joseph V. Edwards

Joseph V. Edwards was born August 22, 1802 in New Jersey. In 1836, Captain Joseph V. Edward's cousin named Cook, for whom Cook County, Illinois was named, returned to New Jersey from Chicago telling of opportunities in the Midwest. Seeking new prosperity in the west, Captain Edwards traveled to Buffalo, New York only to find there was no regular line to get to Chicago. However, he was able to get passage to Detroit on the steamer ROBERT FULTON. After rummaging around Detroit for a while, he worked his way to Green Bay, Wisconsin on a schooner that was delivering supplies to Fort Howard (Green Bay). He remained aboard the schooner bound for Chicago when it stopped to deliver supplies to Conroe's Mill in November 1836. Conroe's Mill was located up the Manitowoc River in Manitowoc Rapids. Land was being cleared at what was to become the city of Manitowoc for a place to load lumber onto schooners for delivery to other Great Lakes ports. The mill was looking for someone to build scows to transport the lumber to the new loading site in Manitowoc. Captain Edwards took the contract to build two scows. The project allowed him to begin his shipbuilding career in Manitowoc. Captain Edwards next went into the fishing business for a few years near the Little Manitowoc River, then into the hotel/tavern business in 1841 in Cooperstown. In 1847 he began construction of the first freighter built in Manitowoc on the north bank of the river just upstream from Riverview Park. Captain Edwards died December 25, 1866.

CITIZEN 1847

Customer – Captain Joseph V. Edwards
Plans and specifications – Wood two-masted schooner – gross tons 54, 60 OM
Final status – Wrecked 6 miles north of Chicago, Illinois, Lake Michigan May 18, 1853
The CITIZEN was the first freight carrying vessel built in Manitowoc.

Manitowoc County Historical Society, INC

CITIZEN

CONVOY 1851

Plans and specifications – Wood schooner – length 65 feet – beam 19.5 feet – depth 5.5 feet – gross tons 64

Bates and Son

Stephen Bates (father) and William W. Bates (son)

Stephen Bates was a master shipwright in New Brunswick, Canada in the 1820s. He and his wife had a son, William, in 1827 and soon after moved to Calais, Maine. Driven by depressed economic conditions, William made trips in 1845 and again in 1848 to the Midwest to find better shipbuilding opportunities. His findings lead the Bates to Manitowoc, Wisconsin in 1851. With Stephen's experience and William's already established ship design skills, the father and son team immediately established Bates and Son shipyard on the Manitowoc River, east of the 8th Street bridge. In 1854, William left the yard for a four year publishing collaboration with his mentor, Marine Architect John Griffiths, in New York City. He did return to Manitowoc to help his father and their yard best he could. In1855, the yard was relocated to the south side of the Manitowoc River between 8th and 9th Streets. However, by 1857 economic depression once again hounded the shipbuilding business. Through the yard's reputation for quality vessels, the Bates and Son yard won contracts for two steamers in 1860 from Captain Albert E. Goodrich. In 1864, the Bates' sold their yard to Greenleaf S. Rand and left for Chicago.

Wisconsin Maritime Museum

William W. Bates

CHALLENGE 1852   Official No. 4349

    Customer – Jarvis E. and O. H. Platt

    Plans and specifications – Wood two-masted schooner with center board – length 85 feet – beam 22.4 feet – depth 6.5 feet – gross tons 87, 110 OM – net tons 83. The pivoting retractable centerboard and flatter bottom aft allowed the CHALLENGE to enter the many undredged harbors of the upper Great Lakes, opening up business previously unserviceable by deeper vessels. Her special hull form also made her capable of 13 miles per hour. This design became a special feature of many more Bates vessels.

    Final status – Beached to a total loss 12 miles south of Sheboygan, Wisconsin, Lake Michigan September 5, 1910

Wisconsin Maritime Museum

CHALLENGE

MARY STOCKTON 1853   Official No. 50515

    Customer – George A. Gibb and Co.

    Plans and specifications – Wood three-masted bark – two center boards – length 140 feet – beam 29 feet – depth 9.6 feet – gross tons 275, 350 OM – net tons 222

    Log – Re-measured – length 144 feet – gross tons – 233 June 2, 1866 – rig changed to barge Port Huron, Michigan April 25, 1867

    Final status – last record December 1890

NORTH YUBA 1853
> Customer – Ezra Durgin Esq.
> Plans and specifications – Wood two-masted topsail schooner with center board length 95 feet – beam 25 feet – depth 6.5 feet – gross tons 140

MARY C. PLATT 1853
> Customer – James Hughes
> Plans and specifications – Wood schooner – gross tons 25

BLACKHAWK 1853
> Plans and specifications – Wood schooner – gross tons 110

COLONEL GLOVER 1853   Official No. 4570
> May have been built by Elias Sorensen
> Customer – M. F. Van Vleck
> Plans and specifications – Wood two-masted schooner – length 84 feet – beam 22.2 feet – depth 7.8 feet – gross tons 89, 107 OM
> Final status – dismantled 1878

CLIPPER CITY 1854   Official No. 4347
> Customer – Jarvis E. and O. H. Platt
> Plans and specifications – Wood two-masted topsail schooner with center board – length 102 feet – beam 27.8 feet – depth 7.5 feet – gross tons 126 – net tons 120. Her refined hull form based on the CHALLENGE, along with her size and rig made her capable of an astonishing 20 miles per hour. This performance became the source of her name and became a long used nickname of the city of Manitowoc.
> Final status – Sank and abandoned North Branch of the Chicago River, Chicago, Illinois June 29, 1895

Wisconsin Maritime Museum

CLIPPER CITY

A north pier, located off the lighthouse, was built between 1852 and 1854 by K. K. Jones and Captain Rouse. A fog bell was placed at the mouth of the river.

STEPHEN BATES 1856   Official No. 22241

    Customer – VanValkenburgh and Company
    Plans and specifications – Wood Schooner with center boards – length 97 feet – beam 27.3 feet – depth 7.5 feet – gross tons 139, 173 OM. The Stephen Bates had a fuller hull form providing more cargo capacity but with slower speed.
    Final status – Grounded, ashore, total loss Lake Michigan, off Winnetka, Illinois, 1883

BELLE 1856   Official No. 2242

    Customer – Lyman Emerson and VanValkenburgh and Company
    Plans and specifications – Wood two-masted brig. schooner – length 91 feet – beam 24.5 feet – depth 6.2 feet – gross tons 123
    Log – July 26, 1858 Captain Edwards brought the schooner BELLE into the Manitowoc River and scuttled her. The captain had more rats then he wanted and he took the plunge to get rid of them.
    Re-measured – gross tons 102 May 12, 1856
    Re-measured – length – 94 feet – depth 7 feet – gross tons 118 – net tons 112
    Re-measured – gross tons 104 – net tons 98
    Final status – Grounded off Big Sable Point, Lake Michigan December 11, 1908

Wisconsin Maritime Museum

BELLE

The 1839 lighthouse was rebuilt taller and with a fifth order lens in 1859.

Chapter 1: Early Freighters and Other Major Shipbuilding 1847 to 1951

UNION 1861Official No. 25048

    Customer – Goodrich Transit Company
    Plans and specifications – Wood freight and passenger steamer – length 163 feet
        – beam 26 feet – depth 10.8 feet – gross tons 435, 553 OM – cost $19,000
    Engine – from the OGONTZ, an earlier Goodrich steamer
    Re-measured – length 166 feet – beam 28.5 feet – gross tons 554 May 22, 1865
    Final status – Ashore Au Sable Point, Lake Superior September 15, 1873

Historical Collection of the Great Lakes, Bowling Green State University
UNION

VICTOR 1861

    Customer – Goodrich Transit Company
    Plans and specifications – Wood side screw wheel freight and passenger steamer
        – length 169 feet – beam 23.6 feet – depth 10.3 feet – gross tons 398 – cost
        $50,000
    Engines – Two steam Peter Murry with Whittaker side propellers
    Re-engined – walking beam 42 inch bore x 120 inch stroke – Detroit Locomotive
        Works – side propellers replaced with side wheels 1862
    Renamed SUNBEAM 1862
    Final status- Foundered 24 miles west of Copper Harbor, Michigan, Lake Superior
        August 28, 1863

Inland Seas Maritime Museum

SUNBEAM

SEA GEM 1863 — Official No. 22582

Customer – Jonah Richards & N. A. Harris

Plans and specifications – Wood two-masted schooner – length 91 feet – beam 22.4 feet – depth 8 feet – gross tons 103, 150 OM – net tons 98

Final status – Wrecked south of Manitowoc breakwater, Lake Michigan September 9, 1901

Great Lakes Marine Collection of the Milwaukee Public Library/Wisconsin Marine Historical Society

SEA GEM

Elias Sorensen

>Elias Sorensen was born in Krager, Norway on January 30, 1825. Elias immigrated to the United States and settled in Manitowoc, Wisconsin in 1849. Trained as a naval architect and ship builder, he established a shipyard soon after arriving in Manitowoc. As his yard was getting under way, he married Jacobine Kullevig in 1851. His yard was located on the east side of the 8th Street bridge. After establishing shipyards in numerous locations throughout the country, Elias died in Chicago, Illinois on August 10, 1911.

Manitowoc County Historical Society, INC

Elias Sorensen

TOLEDO 1852   Official No. 24234

>Customer – C. Anderson
>Plans and specifications – Wood two-masted schooner – length 69 feet – beam 21 feet – depth 6.7 feet – gross tons 100
>Log – Lengthened to 109 feet, third mast added 1866
>   Stranded near Straits of Mackinac September 16, 1869
>Final status – last record 1878

LOMIRA 1853

>Plans and specifications – Wood schooner – gross tons 120 OM

COLONEL GLOVER 1853   Official No. 4570

>May have been built by Bates & Son
>Customer – M. F. VanVleck
>Plans and specifications – Wood two-masted schooner – length 99 feet – beam 24.5 feet – depth 8 feet – gross tons 200
>Final status – dismantled 1878

E. M. SHOYER 1854/5   Official No. 7307

    Customer – John C. Johnson
    Plans and specifications – Wood schooner – length 80 feet – beam 23 feet – depth 6.5 – gross tons 120

ANNIE THORINE 1855   Official No. 569

    Customer – Hans Chios and John Anderson
    Plans and specifications – Wood two-masted schooner – length 80 feet – beam 20.6 feet – depth 6.5 feet – gross tons 93
    Re-measured – gross tons 69 April 14, 1865
    Re-measured – gross tons 89 – net tons 85 May 8, 1875
    Final status – Lost in collision January 24, 1898

Historical Collection of the Great Lakes, Bowling Green State University

ANNIE THORINE

NORTH STAR 1855

Customer – M. F. Van Vleck

Plans and specifications – Wood two-masted schooner – length 108 feet – beam 24.5 feet – depth 8.8 feet – gross tons 175, 208 OM

Log – First sailing vessel to traverse the Soo Locks in Sault Ste. Marie, Michigan June 18, 1855

Final status – Burned in Cleveland, Ohio, Lake Erie February 22, 1862

Inland Seas Maritime Museum

NORTHSTAR

GUIDO 1856   Official No. 10344

Customer – Pfister and Company

Plans and specifications – Wood two-masted schooner – length 103 feet – beam 24.2 feet – depth 7.5 feet – gross tons 146 – net tons 139

Re-measured – length 100 feet – beam 29.5 feet – depth 7.7 feet – gross tons 147 – net tons 139 March 31, 1865

Re-measured – length 115 feet – beam 24.5 feet – depth 7.3 feet – gross tons 136 – net tons 129 May 2, 1891

Log – Sold Canadian April, 1909

Final status – Dropped from Canadian listing 1939

Historical Collection of the Great Lakes, Bowling Green State University
GUIDO

Rand and Harbridge

This shipyard was a partnership between Hanson Rand and James Harbridge. James Harbridge moved from New England to Two Rivers, Wisconsin in 1852.

WILLIAM M. JONES 1853   Official No. 2621

   Customer – K. K. Jones
   Plans and specifications – Wood two-masted clipper schooner – length 108 feet
      – beam 26.0 feet – depth 8.0 feet – gross tons 154, 210 OM – net tons 146
   Final status – Stranded Manitou Islands, Lake Michigan, November 22, 1890

GESINE 1853   Official No. 10333

   Customer – Anderson, Johnson and Captain Simpson
   Plans and specifications – Wood two-masted schooner – length 78.8 feet – beam 23.5
      feet – depth 7.4 feet – gross tons 99 – net tons 94
   Final status – Wrecked Michigan City, Indiana, Lake Michigan, 1887

Hanson Rand

Hanson Rand was born February 21, 1804. He moved to Manitowoc in the late 1840s and established his yard on the Manitowoc River at the northwest corner of the 8th Street bridge. Two of Hanson's sons, E. H. and E. K. Rand, joined their father in the shipbuilding business in 1851. Hanson Rand was Manitowoc Harbor Commissioner in 1865. He died July 20, 1874.

TRANSIT 1854   Official No. 24231

Customer – B. Jones and Company

Plans and specifications – Wood two-masted schooner – length 82 feet – beam 23 feet – depth 7.0 feet – gross tons 92 – net tons 88

Rebuilt at Bates and Sons 1861

Final status – Foundered off Kewaunee, Wisconsin, Lake Michigan September 23, 1891

Great Lakes Marine Collection of the Milwaukee Public Library/Wisconsin Marine Historical Society

TRANSIT

Greenleaf S. Rand

Son of Hanson Rand, Greenleaf was born in Golden Hill, Connecticut May 4, 1830. After learning shipbuilding in Sackett's Harbor, New York, he worked in shipbuilding in St. Louis, Missouri from 1848 to 1849. Around 1854, he moved to Manitowoc, Wisconsin where he established a yard on the south side of the river just east of the 8th Street bridge. Greenleaf was married in 1862. Along with Albert E. Goodrich, Greenleaf established and managed another yard located on the north side of the river west of the 10th Street bridge where vessels were built for the Goodrich Transit Company. In 1870, Greenleaf and Jonah Richards built a recessed dry dock. Greenleaf S. Rand went on to build a total of 33 sailing vessels and 26 steamers.

Wisconsin Maritime Museum

Greenleaf S. Rand

H. RAND 1856   Official No. 11185

Built jointly by Hanson Rand and Greenleaf S. Rand
Customer – Chancy Parker
Plans and specifications – Wood two-masted schooner – length 87 feet – beam 23.4 feet – depth 7.5 feet – gross tons 94, 134 OM
Rebuilt to length 107 feet – beam 23.4 feet – depth 7.5 feet – gross tons 125 – net tons 119 – added third mast 1879
Final status – Foundered off Racine, Wisconsin, Lake Michigan, May 24, 1901 beached and abandoned May 29, 1901

Inland Seas Maritime Museum

H. RAND

A. BAENSCH 1857   Official No. 564

Customer – August Baensch
Plans and specifications – Wood two-masted schooner – length 100 feet – beam 26 feet – depth 8.6 feet – gross tons 197

TRIAL 1857

Plans and specifications – Wood schooner – gross tons 36
Final status – Wrecked November, 1883

EL TEMPO 1857   Official No. 7515

May have been built by S. Goodwin
Customer – Perry P. Smith and Benjamin Jones
Plans and specifications – Wood schooner – length 108 feet – beam 26 feet – depth 8.0 feet – gross tons 166, 215 OM – net tons 158
Final status – Stricken from US registry 1888

JO VILAS 1857   Official No. 12767

   James Harbridge may have been involved in this construction.

   Customer – Greenleaf S. Rand, E. K. Rand and H. C. Albrecht

   Plans and specifications – Wood two-masted schooner – length 107 feet – beam 26 feet – depth 8.8 feet – gross tons 281

   Final status – Foundered 30 miles off Kenosha, Wisconsin, Lake Michigan October 9, 1876

CHICAGO BOARD OF TRADE 1863   Official No. 4331

   Customer – Platt and Vilas and Foster and Harlenberger

   Plans and specifications – Wood three-masted bark – length 157 feet – beam 30.8 feet – depth 13.2 feet – gross tons 423 – net tons 402

   Log – Rig changed to schooner Milwaukee, Wisconsin March 26, 1878

   Final status – Stranded Niagara Reef, Lake Erie, November 21, 1900 – broke up November 26, 1900

Great Lakes Marine Collection of the Milwaukee Public Library/Wisconsin Marine Historical Society
CHICAGO BOARD OF TRADE

NABOB 1864   Official No. 18175

   Customer – F. H. Herd

   Plans and specifications – Wood three-masted schooner – length 138 feet – beam 26.5 feet – depth 11.6 feet – gross tons 310

   Rebuilt and renamed WAUKESHA 1880.

   Final status – Foundered off Muskegon, Michigan, Lake Michigan November 7, 1896

Great Lakes Marine Collection of the Milwaukee Public Library/Wisconsin Marine Historical Society
WAUKESHA

From 1866 through 1872 the harbor mouth was dredged to 13 feet allowing larger ships to conveniently enter the Manitowoc River from Lake Michigan. This increased the shipping commerce and thus increased the demand for more and larger ships to carry freight.

ORION 1866   Official No. 18917

   Customer – Goodrich Transit Company
   Plans and specifications – Wood side wheel freight and passenger steamer – length
      185 feet – beam 28 feet, 48 feet over wheels – depth 11.5 feet – gross tons 495
      – cost $68,000
   Engine – Low pressure walking beam from the MICHIGAN
   Final status – Wrecked Grand Haven, Michigan, Lake Michigan October 16, 1870

NORTHWEST 1867   Official No. 18107

   Customer – Goodrich Transit Company
   Plans and specifications – Wood side wheel freight and passenger steamer – length
      236 feet – beam 32 feet, 58 feet over wheels – depth 13.5 feet – gross tons
      1109 – net tons 754 – cost $117,000
   Engine – Transferred from the PLANET – low pressure vertical beam – 60 inch bore
      X 120 inch stroke – James Murphy, New York
   1000 people attended the launch
   Rebuilt as a day boat and renamed GREYHOUND 1886
   Re-engined – vertical beam 60 inch bore X 144 inch stroke – 1100 horsepower
      – Sheperd Iron Works Buffalo, NY 1899
   Log – Converted to a barge April, 1902 – sank Detroit, Michigan 1904 – raised June
      6, 1905
   Final status – Abandoned Detroit, Michigan June, 1907

Great Lakes Marine Collection of the Milwaukee Public Library/Wisconsin Marine Historical Society

NORTHWEST

MANITOWOC 1867/8   Official No. 90465

    Customer – Goodrich Transit Company

    Plans and specifications – Wood side wheel freight and passenger steamer – length 210 feet – beam 29 feet, 52 feet over wheels – depth 13 feet – gross tons 569 – cost $91,300

    Engine – From MAY QUEEN – low pressure vertical beam condensing 46 inch bore X 132 inch stroke – 450 horsepower – Fletcher & Co. Hoboken, New Jersey

    The MANITOWOC was fast for her day, running from Milwaukee, Wisconsin to Chicago, Illinois in 5 hours and 45 minutes on July 2, 1868, averaging 16 mph. However, this performance was not without cost. Her fine hull and lack of ballast gave her speed but also allowed her to roll excessively, disconcerting many passengers. This, along with a fire caused her to be replaced after only five years of service.

    Log – Super structure burned and dismantled 1873/1874
        Cut down to a wood freight barge – gross tons 507 – net tons 480 September, 1879

    Final status – Waterlogged, July 1, 1900 – wrecked and abandoned, Erie, Pennsylvania Harbor November 10, 1900

SHEBOYGAN 1869   Official No. 115119

    Customer – Goodrich Transportation Company

    Plans and specifications – Wood side wheel freight and passenger steamer – length 209 feet – beam 32 feet, 50 feet over wheels – depth 12 feet – gross tons 624 – net tons 461 – cost $93,300

    Engine – Transferred from steamer CITY OF CLEVELAND – walking beam – condensing – 50 inch bore X 144 inch stroke – 400 horsepower – Buffalo Steam Engine Works Buffalo, New York 1851 – wheels 27 feet X 8 feet

    The Sheboygan's empty hull was towed to Detroit, Michigan where her engines, boilers and cabins were installed, then run back to Manitowoc for completion.

    Log – rebuilt 1896

    Final status – Burned Manitowoc, Wisconsin, Lake Michigan September 24, 1914

Wisconsin Maritime Museum

SHEBOYGAN

CORONA 1869/70   Official No. 125091

    Customer – Goodrich Transportation Company
    Plans and specifications – Wood side wheel freight and passenger steamer – length 172 feet – beam 45 feet – depth 11 feet – gross tons 470 – net tons 374 – cost $42,000
    Engine – Low pressure walking beam – came from Steamer COMET
    Final status – Burned Tonawanda, New York, Niagara River November 17, 1898

Inland Seas Maritime Museum

CORONA

Beginning in 1870, new north and south side piers were begun as a multi-government project and progressed slowly throughout their completion to 1620 feet and 1550 feet into the lake in 1885 and 1887 respectively.

NAVARINO 1870/1   Official No. 18703

Customer – Goodrich Transportation Company
Plans and specifications – Wood freight and passenger steamer – length 184 feet – beam 35.0 feet – depth 12.0 feet – gross tons 760 – cost $60,100
Engine – Steeple compound – 21 inch, 42 inch bore X 36 inch stroke – 950 horsepower C. F. Elmes, Chicago, Illinois
Launched – July 1870 – towed to Chicago, Illinois on July 25, 1870 for machinery installation. The NAVARINO was towed back to Manitowoc, Wisconsin for completion.
Final status – Burned Chicago, Illinois, Chicago River, October 9, 1871 in the great Chicago Fire

Inland Seas Maritime Museum

NAVARINO

MUSKEGON 1871   Official No. 90466

Customer – Goodrich Transit Company
Plans and specifications – Wood side wheel freight and passenger steamer – length 193 feet – beam 29 feet, 46 feet over wheels – depth 12 feet – gross tons 618 – net tons 485 – cost $69,500
Engine – Walking beam from ORION
Log – Wrecked when blocking collapsed at Milwaukee Dry Dock Company Milwaukee, Wisconsin, September 22, 1896
Final Status – Dismantled, hull beached north of Manitowoc, Wisconsin, Lake Michigan 1905

Great Lakes Marine Collection of the Milwaukee Public Library/Wisconsin Marine Historical Society

MUSKEGON

MENOMINEE 1872   Official No. 90720

Customer – Goodrich Transit Company

Plans and specifications – Wood freight and passenger steamer – length 184 feet – beam 34.0 feet – depth 11.0 feet – gross tons 796 – net tons 712 – cost $60,600

Engine – From NAVARINO Steeple compound – 21 inch, 42 inch bores X 36 inch stroke – 950 horsepower – C. F. Elmes, Chicago, Illinois

Log – Full length cabins added 1874

       New arches and upper works 1891

Final status – Remanufactured into the IOWA 1896

Inland Seas Maritime Museum

MENOMINEE

OCONTO 1872   Official No. 19369
    Customer – Goodrich Transit Company
    Plans and specifications – Wood freight and passenger steamer – length 143 feet
        – beam 32.8 feet – depth 10 feet – gross tons 505 – net tons 447 – cost
        $42,200
    Engine – 2 cylinder steam from the steamer SKYLARK.
    Log – Re-engined, re-boilered and added upper deck 1884.
        Grounded Charity Island, Saginaw Bay, Lake Huron December 4, 1885
        – raised and repaired.
    Final status – Struck Granite Rock Shoal and sank at Fisher's Landing, New York, St.
        Lawrence River July 6, 1886

Great Lakes Marine Collection of the Milwaukee Public Library/Wisconsin Marine Historical Society
OCONTO

GEORGE MURRAY 1873   Official No. 85305
    Customer – J. R. Slawson
    Plans and specifications – Wood three-masted schooner – length 203 feet – beam 34
        feet – depth 13.8 feet – gross tons 790 – net tons 750
    Log – Damaged in collision 1880
        Renamed GEORGE 1883

Henry B. Burger

    Henry B. Burger was born on December 14, 1839 in Badhomberg, Germany. He immigrated to America with his parents in December 1846 and settled in Jeffersonville Sullivan County, New York where he grew up on the family farm. He moved to Milwaukee in 1856 and in 1857, he apprenticed at a shipyard becoming a shipwright. He moved to Manitowoc, Wisconsin in 1860 and married Mary Esslinger in 1863. In 1866 he went to Menominee, Michigan to build a scow, then returned to Manitowoc in 1867. He returned to Milwaukee in 1870 where he and his nephew George B. Burger worked at the Wolff and Davidson Shipyard until returning to Manitowoc in 1872.

Wisconsin Maritime Museum
Henry B. Burger

FLEETWING 1867   Official No. 9883

Customer – S. Goddenow and Peter Johnson
Plans and specifications – Wood two-masted schooner – length 145 feet – beam 28.5 feet – depth 11.6 feet – gross tons 350 – cost $30,000
Log – Rebuilt 1885, third mast added
        Ran aground on Green Island, Green Bay, Lake Michigan September 10, 1888
Final status – Stranded in Garrett Bay, Green Bay, Lake Michigan, September 26, 1888 – broke up September 30, 1888

Great Lakes Marine Collection of the Milwaukee Public Library/Wisconsin Marine Historical Society
FLEETWING

S. A. Wood 1868   Official No. 23765

    Customer – Lockwood
    Plans and specifications – Wood three-masted barque – length 150 feet – beam 28 feet – depth 9 feet – gross tons 314 – net tons 298
    Rig changed to schooner in Cleveland, Ohio, April 23, 1878
    Log – Lost mast in a storm on Lake Michigan November 13, 1904
    Final status – Foundered Chicago River, Chicago, Illinois, June 1904

HENRY C. RICHARDS 1873   Official No. 95257

    Customer – Jonah Richards
    Plans and specifications – Wood three-masted schooner – length 189 feet – beam 32.7 feet – depth 13 feet – gross tons 700 – net tons 664
    Final status – Foundered 15 miles off Little Sable Point, Lake Michigan October 27, 1895

Great Lakes Marine Collection of the Milwaukee Public Library/Wisconsin Marine Historical Society
HENRY C. RICHARDS

C. C. Barnes 1873   Official No. 125214

    Customer – J. W. Barnes
    Plans and specifications – Wood three-masted schooner – length 172 feet – beam 31.0 feet – depth 12.0 feet – gross tons 583 – net tons 553
    Renamed BARNES and rebuilt into elevator barge 1914
    Renamed TRANSPORT later 1914
    Final status – Dismantled Milwaukee, Wisconsin, 1919

Wisconsin Maritime Museum

C. C. BARNES

Jonah Richards

Jonah Richards was born June 15, 1825 in Monmouthshire, Wales. He immigrated to America in 1851 and settled in Newport News, Virginia. He quickly moved to Troy, New York, then to Milwaukee, Wisconsin, and finally to Manitowoc, Wisconsin in late 1853. He became involved in shipbuilding initially by providing ironwork from his foundry to existing Manitowoc shipbuilders such as William Bates for the Sea Gem in 1863. He began his own shipbuilding in 1867, building non-freight vessels as well as the freighters listed below. However, being more of an entrepreneur than a shipbuilder, he partnered in the ship building business with Henry B. Burger in 1872, then with James Butler in 1880. In 1870, recognizing a great demand for ship repair on the western Great Lakes, Jonah, along with Greenleaf S. Rand and others, formed the Manitowoc Dry Dock Company to build a recessed dry dock measuring 340 feet x 44 feet x 12 feet for vessels of up to 2000 tons. It was located on Luep's Island just west of today's SooLine Bridge (also known as the jackknife bridge). Jonah became president while Greenleaf was appointed general manager. Jonah Richards died September 22, 1881.

ALICE RICHARDS 1867   Official No. 567

   Built in association with Jasper Hanson
   Customer – Jonah Richards
   Plans and specifications – Wood three-masted barque – length 147 feet – beam 27
       feet – depth 10.0 feet – gross tons 286 – net tons 274
   Final status – abandoned 1910

CITY OF MANITOWOC 1872   Official No. 125217

   Built in association with Henry B. Burger
   Customer – Jonah Richards
   Plans and specifications – Wood three-masted schooner – length 138 feet – beam 26.0
       feet – depth 11.5 feet – gross tons 310
   Final status – Wrecked Georgian Bay, Lake Huron – sold foreign between 1876 and 1879

Great Lakes Marine Collection of the Milwaukee Public Library/Wisconsin Marine Historical Society

CITY OF MANITOWOC

BLAZING STAR 1873   Official No. 2868

    Built in association with Henry B. Burger

    Customer – M. J. Cummings
    Plans and specifications – Wood three-masted schooner – length 137 feet – beam 26.0 feet – depth 10.0 feet – gross tons 279 – net tons 265
    Final status – Stranded Fisherman Shoal, Lake Michigan November 12, 1887

MOCKING BIRD 1874   Official No. 90744

    Plans and specifications – Wood three-masted schooner – length 112 feet – beam – 22.2 feet – depth 7.6 feet – gross tons 159 – net tons 151
    Built from previous vessel built in 1851
    Final status – Wrecked Middlesex July 22, 1889

Jasper Hanson and E. W. Packard

JESSIE PHILLIPS 1868   Official No. 75367

    Plans and specifications – Wood two-masted schooner – length 128 feet – beam 26 feet – depth 8 feet – gross tons 198 – net tons 177
    Final status – Abandoned 1903

Jasper Hanson

    Jasper Hanson was born in Denmark on January 5, 1832 and immigrated to America in 1854 and settled in Manitowoc, Wisconsin. He worked as a general worker and carpenter until 1866 when he started his own shipyard with help from Alonzo D. Jones. His yard was located near Jones's mill east of the 8th Street bridge and employed about seventy men.

LOUISA MCDONALD 1869   Official No. 15872

    Customer – Alonzo D. Jones, Jasper Hanson, D. J. Easton
    Plans and specifications – Wood two-masted schooner – length 124 feet – beam 25.6
        feet – depth 8.0 feet – gross tons 192 – net tons 182
    Log – Added third mast Chicago, Illinois April 1877
        Beached May 20, 1883 Milwaukee, Wisconsin, Lake Michigan
    Rebuilt and renamed LILY E. June 1, 1883
    South Shore Yacht Club Milwaukee, Wisconsin club house 1915
    Final status – Burned Milwaukee Harbor September 1922

Great Lakes Marine Collection of the Milwaukee Public Library/Wisconsin Marine Historical Society
LOUISA MCDONALD

H. C. ALBRECHT 1870   Official No. 95135

Plans and specifications – Wood two-masted schooner – length 132 feet – beam 26.3 feet – depth 8.4 feet – gross tons 210 – net tons 199
Renamed THOMAS HUME, November 21, 1883
Final status – Foundered out of Chicago, Illinois for Muskegon, Michigan, Lake Michigan May 21, 1891

J. A. STORNACH 1870   Official No. 12978

Customer – J. A. Stornach
Rebuilt from a vessel built by George Barber in Milwaukee, Wisconsin in 1854
Plans and specifications – Wood three-masted schooner – length 110 feet – beam 24 feet – depth 7.0 feet – gross tons 143 – net tons 136
Renamed A.B.C.F.M. October 10, 1881
Final status – Abandoned and sank Milwaukee, Wisconsin 1902

Great Lakes Marine Collection of the Milwaukee Public Library/Wisconsin Marine Historical Society
A.B.C.F.M.

J. B. NEWLAND 1870   Official No. 75366

Built in association with George Henderson

Customer – Burdick
Plans and specifications – Wood two-masted schooner – length 112 feet – beam 26 feet – depth 7.8 feet – gross tons 157 – net tons 149
Rebuilt 1882
Re-rigged – added third mast, Chicago, Illinois July 1887
Final status – Stranded on North Manitou Island shoal, Lake Michigan September 8, 1910 and broke up in storms and ice over time.

Inland Seas Maritime Museum

J. B. NEWLAND

Inland Seas Maritime Museum

J. B. NEWLAND

H. E. MCALLISTER 1870
Plans and specifications – Wood two-masted schooner – gross tons 237

WILLIE KELLER 1871   Official No. 80315
Plans and specifications – Wood three-masted schooner – length 134 feet – beam 25 feet – depth 9.0 feet – gross tons 236 – net tons 224
Final status – Sank in a collision off AuSable Point July 1888

E. W. Packard

C. L. JOHNSON 1869   Official No. 5990
Plans and specifications – Wood two-masted schooner – length 123 feet – beam 28.2 feet – depth 7.7 feet – gross tons 199 – net tons 189
Renamed – Z.Y.M.C.A. 1882
Final status – Abandoned 1894

Historical Collection of the Great Lakes, Bowling Green State University
C. L. JOHNSON

Peter Larson

Peter Larson was born in Roverud in Bamle, Norway on July 11, 1829. He came to the United States in 1854 and settled in Manitowoc, Wisconsin where he established a shipyard east of the SooLine Bridge, sometimes known as shipbuilder's point. In 1864, he married Anne Christianson with whom he had fourteen children. Peter Larson died July 11, 1895.

Manitowoc County Historical Society, INC
Peter Larson

ESPINDOLA 1869   Official No. 8792

    Plans and specifications – Wood two-masted schooner – length 60 feet – beam 18.6
        feet – depth 6.0 feet – gross tons 54
    Final status – Wrecked Chicago, Illinois 1892

INDUSTRY 1870   Official No. 100023

    Plans and specifications – Wood two-masted schooner – length 73.5 feet – beam 18.5
        feet – depth 6.0 feet – gross tons 55 – net tons 52
    Log – Sank between Two Rivers and Manitowoc, Wisconsin, Lake Michigan
        December 1871 – raised and repaired
    Final status – Abandoned Sturgeon Bay, Wisconsin, February 1918

GILBERT KNAPP 1871   Official No. 10337

    Rebuild from a vessel built in Racine, Wisconsin by Beckwith in 1854
    Plans and specifications – Wood three-masted schooner – length 119 feet – beam 26
        feet – depth 8 feet – gross tons 186 – net tons 177
    Final status – Grounded Good Harbor Bay, 1896

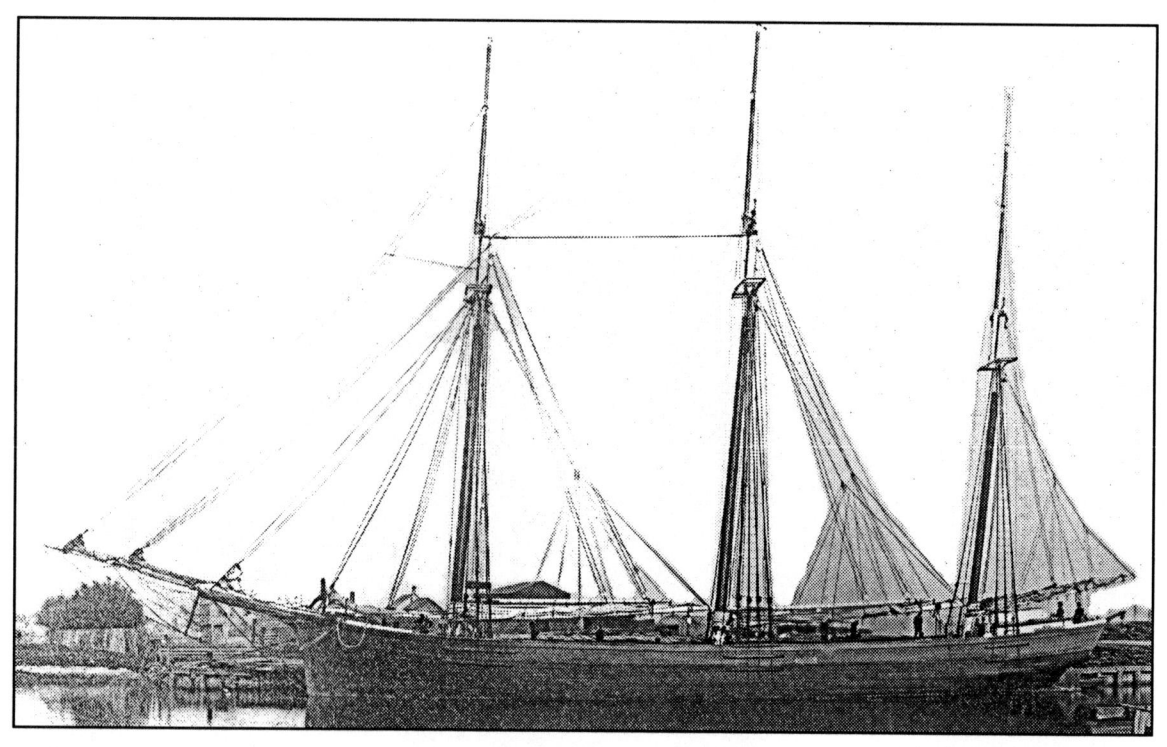

Inland Seas Maritime Museum

GILBERT KNAPP

WILLIS 1872

    Plans and specifications – Wood three-masted schooner – length 132 feet – beam 27.9 feet – depth 9.0 feet – gross tons 260

    Final status – Sank after collision with ELIZABETH JONES off Point Pellee, Lake Erie, fall 1872

FELICITOUS 1873   Official No. 120121

    Plans and specifications – Wood three-masted schooner – length 126 feet – beam 26 feet – depth 7.0 feet – gross tons 199 – net tons 189

    Final status – Abandoned 1913

Chapter 1: Early Freighters and Other Major Shipbuilding 1847 to 1951   33

Manitowoc County Historical Society, INC

FELICITOUS shown in the Burger and Burger floating dry dock in 1888
with other vessels under construction in the background.

Inland Seas Maritime Museum

FELICITOUS

CITY OF WOODSTOCK 1873   Official No. 125223

Plans and specifications – Wood schooner – length 113 feet – beam 25.5 feet – depth 8.3 feet – gross tons 164 – net tons 156

Renamed R. KANTERS and rebuilt deck 1882/83

Final status – Total loss Grand Haven, Michigan June 8, 1896

CHARLES LULING 1873   Official No. 125215

Customer – S. Hall

Plans and specifications – Wood three-masted schooner – length 123 feet – beam 26 feet – depth 9.6 feet – gross tons 214 – net tons 204

Log – Stranded off Manistique, Michigan, Lake Michigan fall 1890 – released spring 1891

Re-measured – gross tons 195 – net tons 185 March 14, 1894

Final status – Stranded east end of Middle Ground, Vineyard Haven, Massachusetts December 12, 1913

Inland Seas Maritime Museum

CHARLES LULING

JULIA LARSON 1874   Official No. 75719

Customer – Peterson

Plans and specifications – Wood two-masted schooner – length 70 feet – beam 18.8 feet – depth 6.4 feet – gross tons 59 – net tons 56

Sold Canadian late 1903

Final status – Stricken from Canadian registry 1933 or 38

Inland Seas Maritime Museum

JULIA LARSON

MERCHANT 1874   Official No. 90616

Plans and specifications – Wood two-masted schooner – length 79.4 feet – beam 19.0 feet – depth 6.5 feet – gross tons 66 – net tons 62

Final status – Wrecked on Racine Reef, total loss, July 1874 or stranded at Sandusky, Ohio, Lake Erie June 28, 1904

Inland Seas Maritime Museum

MERCHANT docked on north side of the Manitowoc River
with Richards Iron Works in the background.

TALLAHASSEE 1881　　　　　　　　　　　　　　Official No. 145249

Plans and specifications – Wood two-masted schooner – length 68 feet – beam 21 feet – depth 6.4 feet – gross tons 83 – net tons 79

Final status – Out of commission 1894

Hanson and Scove

This shipbuilding business was a partnership between Japser Hanson and Hans Scove. Hans M. Scove was born in Denmark on February 15, 1837. He immigrated to the United States in 1855 to Long Island, New York where he learned shipbuilding. He moved to Manitowoc, Wisconsin in 1858. He joined the established yard of Jasper Hanson to form Hanson and Scove in 1868. The yard was moved to Two Rivers, Wisconsin in September 1873, then back to Manitowoc in 1879. Hans Scove died on March 22, 1889. Jasper Hanson died in 1904.

KATE L. BRUCE 1871　　　　　　　　　　　　　Official No. 142772

Plans and specifications – Wood three-masted schooner – gross tons 310

Final status – Foundered Lake Michigan 1877

CHRISTINA NILSSON 1871　　　　　　　　　　Official No. 125293

Customer – Charles M. Lindgren

Plans and specifications – Wood three-masted schooner – length 139 feet – beam 26.0 feet – depth 11.4 feet – gross tons 311

Final status – Stranded outer reef Baileys Harbor, Wisconsin, Lake Michigan October 24, 1884

LOUIS MEEKER 1871/2 — Official No. 15873

    Plans and specifications – Wood schooner – gross tons 312

MARGARET A. MUIR 1872 — Official No. 90459

    Customer – Muir and Clow

    Plans and specifications – Wood three-masted schooner – length 129 feet – beam 26.2 feet – depth 11.5 feet – gross tons 347 – net tons 330

    Final status – Foundered two miles off Algoma, Wisconsin, Lake Michigan September 30, 1893

THOMAS H. HOWLAND 1872 — Official No. 24978

    Customer – Charles M. Lindgren

    Plans and specifications – Wood three-masted schooner – length 139 feet – beam 26.2 feet – depth 11.1 feet – gross tons 299 – net tons 283

    Final status – Abandoned 1921

MARY L. HIGGIE 1872 — Official No. 90461

    Customer – J. L. Higgie

    Plans and specifications – Wood three-masted schooner – length 139 feet – beam 26.3 feet – depth 11.2 feet – gross tons 310 – net tons 295

    Log – Collided head on with another schooner in heavy fog off Skillagalee Island, Lake Michigan February 5, 1879, but continued on

    Renamed HATTIE A. ESTELL January 19, 1889

    Final status – Broke up and sank in a storm off Manistee pier Manistee, Michigan, Lake Michigan November 17, 1891

FALMOUTH 1873 — Official No. 24984

    Customer – Turner and Keller

    Plans and specifications – Wood three-masted schooner – gross tons 234

    Final status – Collided with Buffalo breakwater and sank, Buffalo, New York, Lake Erie November 21, 1880

GUIDO PFISTER 1873 — Official No. 85304

    Plans and specifications – Wood three-masted schooner – length 198 feet – beam 33 feet – depth 13.2 feet – gross tons 694 – net tons 661

    Final status – Stranded on pier at harbor entrance Duluth, Minnesota, Lake Superior October 10, 1885

Historical Collection of the Great Lakes, Bowling Green State University
GUIDO PFISTER

H. M. SCOVE 1873 — Official No. 95256

Plans and specifications – Wood three-masted schooner – length 130 feet – beam 26 feet – depth 10.0 feet – gross tons 305 – net tons 290

Final status – Sank between Pilot Island and Detroit Island, Deaths Door, Lake Michigan December 5, 1891

DAISY DAY 1880 — Official No. 157002

Customer – John Jacobs and George B. Guyles

Plans and specifications – Wood steam barge – length 103 feet – beam 20.7 feet – depth 7.6 feet – gross tons 146 – net tons 124

Final status – Stranded at Lees Pier, near Little Sable Point, Lake Michigan October 11, 1891

MELITTA 1881　　　　　　　　　　　　　　　　　Official No. 91309

　　Customer – H. Jensen or Seymour
　　Plans and specifications – Wood two-masted schooner – length 70 feet – beam 20 feet – depth 6.0 feet – gross tons 58 – net tons 54
　　Rebuilt – Length 88 feet – beam 20.5 feet – depth 7.2 feet – gross tons 83 – net tons 79 May, 1879
　　Rebuilt – Depth 5.5 feet – gross tons 68 July, 1905
　　Log – Beached in heavy fog just south of Sheboygan, Wisconsin, Lake Michigan May 14, 1909 – released May 17, 1909
　　Final status – Abandoned Detroit, Michigan 1924

Michigan Maritime Museum Collection

MELITTA

EMILY B. MAXWELL 1881   Official No. 135536

Customer – O. B. Mullin

Plans and specifications – Wood three-masted schooner – length 149 feet – beam 30.9 feet – depth 10.7 feet – gross tons 360 – net tons 343

Sold Canadian 1904

Final status – Stranded off Cleveland breakwater, Lake Erie August 31, 1909

Inland Seas Maritime Museum

EMILY B. MAXWELL

THOMAS L. PARKER 1881   Official No. 145264

    Plans and specifications – Wood three-masted schooner – length 186 feet – beam 33
        feet – depth 13.5 feet – gross tons 628 – net tons 597
    Final status – Abandoned New York, New York 1926

J. LOOMIS MC CLAREN 1882   Official No. 76331

    Plans and specifications – Wood three-masted schooner – length 133 feet – beam 29.0
        feet – depth 9.5 feet – gross tons 292 – net tons 272
    Final status – Wrecked May 1894

EMMA L. NIELSEN 1883   Official No. 135665

    Customer – Captain Paul Nielsen and Hugo J Kleinholz
    Plans and specifications – Wood two-masted schooner – length 74.7 feet – beam 20.6
        feet – depth 6.2 feet – gross tons 62.4 – net tons 59
    Lengthened – 98.2 feet – gross tons 90 – net tons 86 – added third mast Burger and
        Burger 1890
    Final status – Sank in a collision 11 miles off Point Aux Barques, Michigan, Lake
        Huron June 26, 1911

Great Lakes Marine Collection of the Milwaukee Public Library/Wisconsin Marine Historical Society

EMMA L. NIELSEN

LINERLA 1884   Official No. 140732

May have been built by Mads Ornes

Customer – Osul Torrison

Plans and specifications – Wood two-masted schooner – length 78 feet – beam 21.9 feet – depth 6.6 feet – gross tons 77 – net tons 73

Final status – Stricken from registry 1905

JAMES H. HALL 1885   Official No. 76553

Customer – Captain Christ Christiansen

Plans and specifications – Wood two-masted schooner – length 92 feet – beam 22 feet – depth 7 feet – gross tons 100 – net tons 95

Final status – Lost to fire at a pier in Alpena, Michigan, Lake Huron November 7, 1916

Great Lakes Marine Collection of the Milwaukee Public Library/Wisconsin Marine Historical Society

JAMES H. HALL

FRANCIS HINTON 1889　　　　　　　　　　Official No. 120754

Customers – Horatio Truman, George Cooper, and Francis Hinton
Plans and specifications – Wood steam barge lumber hooker – length 152 feet – beam 30.9 feet – depth 10.8 feet – gross tons 417 – net tons 331
Engine – Steeple compound – 19 inch, 36 inch bores X 30 inch stroke – 385 horsepower – Manistee Iron Works, Manistee, Michigan 1889
Final status – Waterlogged and stranded 4 ½ miles south of Two Rivers, Wisconsin, Lake Michigan November 16, 1909

Inland Seas Maritime Museum

FRANCIS HINTON

Inland Seas Maritime Museum

FRANCIS HINTON in dry dock

JOHN E. HALL 1889/90 — Official No. 76790

Samuel Hall may have been involved in this construction.

Customer – Timothy Donovan

Plans and specifications – Wood steamer – length 139 feet – beam 28.6 feet – depth 10.9 feet – gross tons 343 – net tons 279

Final status – Foundered near Duck Islands, Lake Ontario December 13, 1902

Inland Seas Maritime Museum

Launch of the JOHN E. HALL

James Butler

James Butler was born in 1843. He began his first freighter at the age of only 28.

MYSTIC STAR 1873 — Official No. 90534

Customer – M. J. Owinger

Plans and specifications – Wood three-masted schooner – length 139 feet – beam 26 feet – depth 11.8 feet – gross tons 339 – net tons 322

Final status – Sank off Fairhaven, Ohio, Lake Erie 1892

G. C. TRUMPF 1873 — Official No. 85373

Customer – Thomas Windiate and James Butler

Plans and specifications – Wood three-masted schooner – length 136 feet – beam 26.2 feet – depth 11.3 feet – gross tons 347 – net tons 329

Renamed ARTHUR and lengthened to 148 feet – gross tons 335 – net tons 318, May 16, 1885

Sold Canadian, April 8, 1902

Final status – Sank St. Lawrence River, Morrisburg, Ontario August 21, 1917

Historical Collection of the Great Lakes, Bowling Green State University

G. C. TRUMPF

CORNELLIA B. WINDIATE 1874   Official No. 125375

Customer – Thomas Windiate and James Butler

Plans and specifications – Wood three-masted schooner – length 139 feet – beam 26.2 feet – depth 11.6 feet – gross tons 332 – cost $20,000

Final status – Sank north of Middle Island near Alpena, Michigan, Lake Huron November 30, 1875

DAVID VANCE 1874   Official No. 6855

Customers – Hibbard and Vance, W. A. Wilkins, and William Beck
Plans and specifications – Wood three-masted schooner – length 207 feet – beam 33.7 feet – depth 14.4 feet – gross tons 774 – net tons 736
Log – Beached in fog three miles south of Sheboygan, Wisconsin, Lake Michigan June 1, 1875 – released
    Grounded in fog on Lela Shoal, Straits of Mackinaw November 2, 1876 – released
    Collided with the J. B. Penfield in heavy fog off Point Au Sable, Lake Michigan, June 12, 1883 – repaired
    Grounded and sank near the mouth of the Detroit River, Lake Erie June 17, 1886 – raised and repaired
    Collided and sank near Point Pelle, Lake Erie July 20, 1893
Final status – Wreck completely destroyed in heavy gale October 21, 1893

Great Lakes Marine Collection of the Milwaukee Public Library/Wisconsin Marine Historical Society
DAVID VANCE

HENRIETTA ESCH 1877   Official No. 95476

Plans and specifications – Wood two-masted schooner – length 68 feet – beam 18.2 feet – depth 5.8 feet – gross tons 42 – net tons 39
Final status – Foundered Gulf of Mexico after 1886

MAY RICHARDS 1880   Official No. 91283

Customer – Jonah Richards
Plans and specifications – Wood three-masted schooner barge – length 161 feet – beam 27.4 feet – depth 15.5 feet – gross tons 511 – net tons 485
Built from steamer SUSQUEHANNA
Final status – Last record 1906

Inland Seas Maritime Museum

MAY RICHARDS being towed by the RUBE RICHARDS

RUBE RICHARDS 1881   Official No. 110480

Customer – Jonah Richards
Built as an un-powered steamer – schooner rigged to sail to Detroit, Michigan to have the engine and propeller installed.
Plans and specifications – Wood steamer – length 175 feet – beam 33.3 feet – depth 17.7 feet – gross tons 815 – net tons 594
Engine – Steeple compound – 24 inch, 48 inch bores X 36 inch stroke – Frontier Iron Works, Detroit, Michigan
Log – cut down to a barge 1905 – gross tons 815 – net tons 774
Final status – Abandoned June, 1917

Great Lakes Marine Collection of the Milwaukee Public Library/Wisconsin Marine Historical Society

RUBE RICHARDS

LALLAH ROOKH 1881   Official No. 140481
    Plans and specifications – Wood two-masted schooner – length 66 feet – beam 19.3
        feet – depth 6.4 feet – gross tons 60.4 – net tons 57.3
    Final status – Last record 1902

GLAD TIDINGS 1883   Official No. 85788
    Customer – Captain Henry Bundy
    Plans and specifications – Wood two-masted schooner – length 65 feet – beam 20.0
        feet – depth 8.0 feet – gross tons 71
    Rebuilt to length 79 feet – beam 20.0 feet – depth 6.2 feet – gross tons 81 – net tons
        77 Port Huron, Michigan April, 1889
    Final status – Sank after collision with steamer Pathfinder near Fighting Island,
        Detroit River July 29, 1894

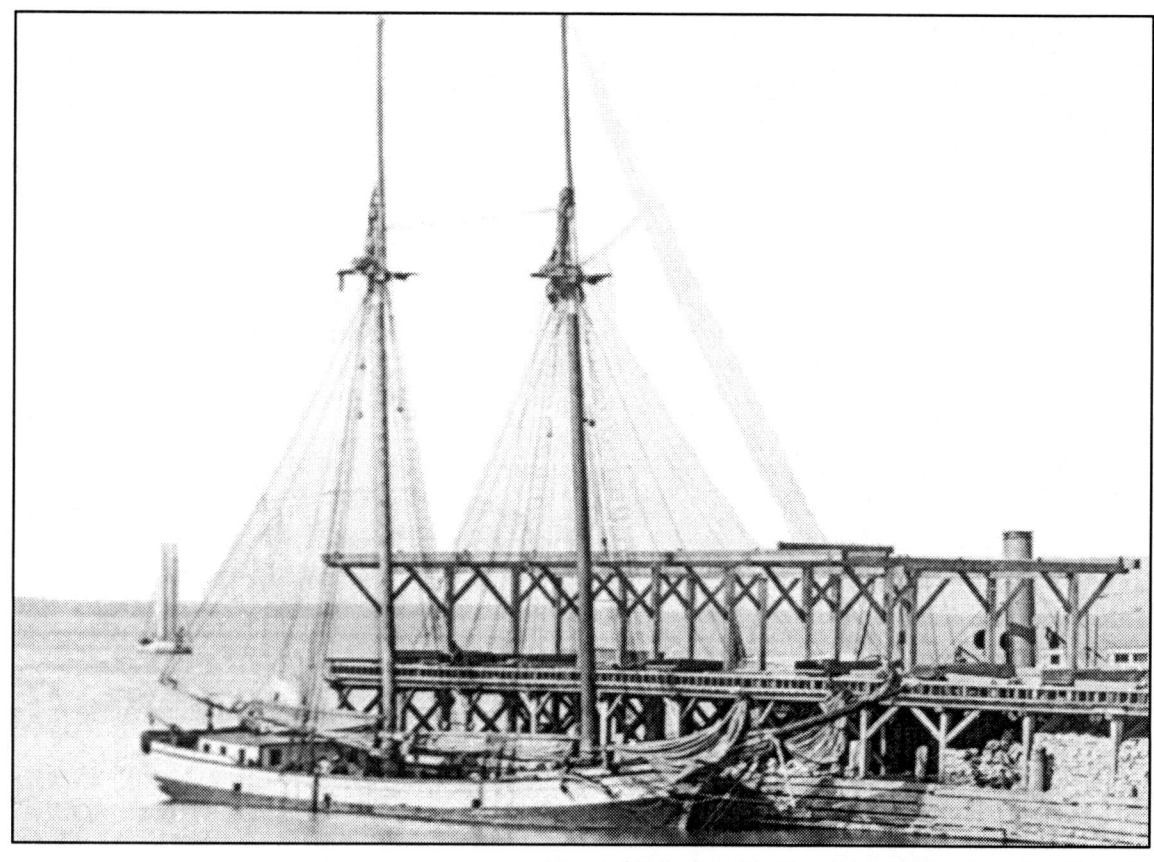

Historical Collection of the Great Lakes, Bowling Green State University
GLAD TIDINGS

James Butler, unable to obtain a shipbuilding contract for his yard in Manitowoc, became yard superintendent at Wolff and Davidson shipyard in Milwaukee in 1885. James Butler died in July of 1888 in Milwaukee, Wisconsin or on July 2, 1888 in Oshkosh, Wisconsin and was buried in Manitowoc.

Mads Ornes

Mads Ornes was born in Vikedal, Norway on September 29, 1834 and immigrated to the United States in 1870 with his wife Marie and five children. Trained in shipbuilding in Norway, he established a small shipyard in Manitowoc. Mads Ornes died, August 18, 1907.

MINNEHAHA 1872   Official No. 90584

    Customer – Osul Torrison

    Plans and specifications – Wood two-masted schooner – length 71 feet – beam 18.4 feet – depth 6.6 feet – gross tons 59 – net tons 56

MISHICOTT 1882   Official No. 91439

    May have been built by Gunder Jorgenson

    Plans and specifications – Wood two-masted schooner – length 79.2 feet – beam 21.5 feet – depth 6.1 feet – gross tons 77 – net tons 73

    Re-measured – gross tons 73 – net tons 69, September 7, 1889

    Final status – Abandoned January 26, 1912

Historical Collection of the Great Lakes, Bowling Green State University
MISHICOTT

LINERLA 1884   Official No. 140732

    May have been built by Hanson and Scove

    Customer – Osul Torrison

    Plans and specifications – Wood two-masted schooner – length 78 feet – beam 21.9 feet – depth 6.6 feet – gross tons 77 – net tons 73

    Final status – Stricken from registry 1905

W. C. KIMBALL 1888   Official No. 81178

    Plans and specifications – Wood two-masted schooner – length 63.3 feet – beam 17.3 feet – depth 4.9 feet – gross tons 33 – net tons 31

    Final status – last record 1891

Larson and Son
>   May have been built by or in conjunction with J. Jones

L. J. CONWAY 1873 — Official No. 15955

>   Plans and specifications – Wood two-masted schooner – length 80.6 feet – beam 21.6 feet – depth 6.4 feet – gross tons 90.5 – net tons 85
>   Log – Struck pier and sank Sheboygan, Wisconsin November 23, 1881 – raised and repaired Beached in a storm Hyde Park, Illinois, Lake Michigan May 23, 1883 – later released
>   Final status – Foundered seven miles north of White Lake near Fowler Creek, Michigan, Lake Michigan November 17, 1886

Rand and Burger
>   Rand and Burger was a partnership between Greenleaf S. Rand and Henry B. Burger. It was formed in 1873 and was located on the south side of Luep's Island near the Sooline Bridge. The property was about nine acres and had 1200 feet of Manitowoc River frontage. There were approximately 100 employees. Rand and Burger became the operator of the recessed dry dock built in 1870 by Greenleaf S. Rand and Jonah Richards.

THISTEL 1873 — Official No. 24979

>   Customer – Captain William Gamble
>   Plans and specifications – Wood three-masted schooner – length 138 feet – beam 26.1 feet – depth 11.6 feet – gross tons 363
>   Final status – last record 1878

DEPERE 1873 — Official No. US6849

>   Customer – Goodrich Transit Company
>   Plans and specifications – Wood freight and passenger steamer – length 165 feet – beam 29 feet – depth 10 feet – gross tons 735 – net tons 639 – cost $57,200
>   Engine – Steeple compound – 22 inch, 40 inch bores X 36 inch stroke – 585 horsepower – Thomas Murphy, Detroit, Michigan 1873
>   Renamed – STATE OF MICHIGAN 1893
>   Log – Wrecked near Two Rivers, Wisconsin, Lake Michigan December 8, 1881 – raised July 1882
>   Final status – Broke connecting rod piercing hull and sank off White Lake, Michigan, Lake Michigan October 18, 1901

Inland Seas Maritime Museum

DEPERE

LYDIA 1873/4   Official No. 140056

    Customer – Schmidt and Wettenberg
    Plans and specifications – Wood two-masted schooner – length 80 feet – beam 20.9 feet – depth 6.8 feet – gross tons 84 – net tons 79
    Final status – Stranded ½ mile south of Manistee, Michigan, Lake Michigan October 20, 1905 – Abandoned there 1907

Great Lakes Marine Collection of the Milwaukee Public Library/Wisconsin Marine Historical Society
LYDIA docked in Racine

CHICAGO 1874   Official 125338

    Customer – Goodrich Transit Company
    Plans and specifications – Wood side wheel freight and passenger steamer – length 205 feet – beam 30 feet, 55 feet over guards – depth 12 feet – gross tons 746 – net tons 589 – cabins from steamer MANITOWOC – cost $85,000
    Engine – Walking beam – condensing – 46 inch bore X 132 inch stroke – 450 horsepower – Fletcher and Company, Hoboken, NJ from steamer MANITOWOC from steamer MAY QUEEN – wheels 26 feet X 8 feet
    Log – Condemned 1915
        Converted to housing by and for Manitowoc Shipbuilding employees, Manitowoc, Wisconsin 1916
    Final status – Abandoned and dismantled, June 30, 1919, burned north of Little Manitowoc River, Lake Michigan August 12, 1919

Wisconsin Maritime Museum

CHICAGO shown when it was nearly new

Great Lakes Marine Collection of the Milwaukee Public Library/Wisconsin Marine Historical Society

CHICAGO exchanging passengers in Milwaukee, circa 1880

Chapter 1: Early Freighters and Other Major Shipbuilding 1847 to 1951   53

Inland Seas Maritime Museum

CHICAGO with a new pilot house and paint scheme, circa 1895

J. I. CASE 1874   Official No. 75720

Customer – J. I. Case Plow Works Company
Plans and specifications – Wood three-masted schooner – length 208 feet – beam 34.5 feet – depth 14.5 feet – gross tons 827 – net tons 786 – main-mast was 190 feet above the water line.
Sold Canadian 1920
Final status – Sank near Quebec City, Quebec, St. Lawrence River fall 1933

Inland Seas Maritime Museum

J. I. CASE

Wisconsin Maritime Museum

J. I. CASE in dry dock

J. DUVALL 1874   Official No. 75721

    Customer – George W. Slauson
    Plans and specifications – Wood two-masted schooner – length 103 feet – beam 24.3
        feet – depth 7.6 feet – gross tons 131 – net tons 125 – cost $7000
    Namesake – Joseph Duvall
    Log – Capsized off Two Rivers, Wisconsin, Lake Michigan July 9, 1880 – raised
    Final status – Sank after collision with JAMES B. COLGATE near Tashmoo Island,
        Ontario, St. Clair River December 5, 1905

Inland Seas Maritime Museum

J. DUVALL

H. B. BURGER 1875 — Official No. 95367

Plans and specifications – Wood schooner – length 118 feet – beam 26 feet – depth 9.0 feet – gross tons 190 – net tons 181

Final status – Wrecked against breakwater off Twenty-Eighth Street, Chicago, Illinois, Lake Michigan May 22, 1883

J. V. JONES 1875 — Official No. 75766

Customer – Thomas Jones

Plans and specifications – Wood three-masted schooner – length 125 feet – beam 22.0 feet – depth 9.1 feet – gross tons 236 – net tons 224

Namesake – John V. Jones

Final status – Lost January 1906

LUCIA A. SIMPSON 1875 — Official No. 140097

Customer – Wellingford E. Simpson, Simpson and Company

Plans and specifications – Wood three-masted schooner – length 127 feet – beam 28 feet – depth 8.7 feet – gross 227 – net tons 215

Final status – Burned Sturgeon Bay, Wisconsin December 3, 1935

Great Lakes Marine Collection of the Milwaukee Public Library/Wisconsin Marine Historical Society
LUCIA A. SIMPSON on the south side of the Manitowoc River
with the Tenth Street bridge in the background.

LOTTIE COOPER 1876   Official No. 140185

    Customer – Jones and Cooper
    Plans and specifications – Wood three-masted schooner – length 131 feet – beam 27
        feet – depth 9.0 feet – gross tons 252 – net tons 232
    Final status – Wrecked just south of Sheboygan, Wisconsin, Lake Michigan April 9,
        1894

Great Lakes Marine Collection of the Milwaukee Public Library/Wisconsin Marine Historical Society
LOTTIE COOPER

ISAAC WATSON STEPHENSON 1879   Official No. 100244

    Customer – Kirby Carpenter Company
    Plans and specifications – Wood three-masted schooner barge – length 163 feet
        – beam 32 feet – depth 11.0 feet – gross 462 – net tons 439
    Rebuilt – Sorel, Quebec Canada 1915
    Final status – Abandoned and dismantled about 1932 – ended registry 1935

PENOBSCOT 1880   Official No. 150193

    Plans and specifications – Wood three-masted schooner – length 134 feet – beam 27.4
        feet – depth 9.2 feet – gross 257 – net tons 244
    Converted to a steam barge 1908
    Converted to a sand dredge 1911
    Final status – Burned Marine City, Michigan August 19, 1925

Great Lakes Marine Collection of the Milwaukee Public Library/Wisconsin Marine Historical Society

PENOBSCOT

CITY OF LUDINGTON 1880   Official No. 125873

Customer – Goodrich Transit Company

Plans and specifications – Wood freight and passenger steamer – length 180 feet – beam 35.4 feet – depth 12.0 feet – gross tons 842 – net tons 738 – cost $60,000

Engine – Reynolds-Corliss – high pressure – 24 inch bore X 36 inch stroke, 325 horsepower – Edward P. Allis, Milwaukee, Wisconsin

Log – Stranded Shanty Bay Green Bay, Lake Michigan, November 24, 1888 released spring of 1889

Final status – Rebuilt and renamed GEORGIA by Burger and Burger 1898

Inland Seas Maritime Museum

CITY OF LUDINGTON

S. M. STEPHENSON 1880   Official No. 115722

    Customer – Kirby Carpenter Company
    Plans and specifications – Wood three-masted schooner barge – length 166 feet
        – beam 33.0 feet – depth 12.0 feet – gross 512 – net tons 459
    Rebuilt as a steam barge in Grand Haven, Michigan 1901 – gross tons 546 – net tons 426
    Engine – High pressure – 25 inch bore X 30 inch stroke – Cuyahoga Iron Works
        Cleveland, Ohio from steam barge CLEVELAND
    Re-engined - Fore and aft compound – 20 inch, 40 inch bores X 30 inch stroke
        – Montague Iron Works, Montague, Michigan 1901
    Final status – Abandoned Bay City, Michigan 1935

Wisconsin Maritime Museum

S. M. STEPHENSON

HENRY WHITBECK 1880   Official No. 95590

    Customer – O. R. Johnson
    Plans and specifications – Wood three-masted schooner barge – length 167 feet
        – beam 33.1 feet – depth 11.0 feet – gross tons 498 – net tons 473
    Sold Canadian 1917

IMPERIAL 1881   Official No. 100270

    Plans and specifications – Wood steamer – length 89 feet – beam 19 feet – depth 4.8
        feet – gross tons 68 – net tons 43
    Final status – Wrecked Surprise Shoal, Georgian Bay, Lake Huron 1889

Inland Seas Maritime Museum

IMPERIAL

A. A. CARPENTER 1881   Official No. 105978

Customer – Kirby Carpenter Company

Plans and specifications – Wood three-masted schooner barge – length 165 feet – beam 33.0 feet – depth 12.2 feet – gross tons 540 – net tons 524

Rebuilt as an elevator and renamed COLLIER May 1918

Remodeled into a showboat and renamed COTTON BLOSSOM for the Chicago World's Fair 1933. Later it became a dance hall and gambling den and was raided numerous times and renamed SHOW BOAT SAM.

Log – Burned Chicago River February 19, 1936

Final status – Towed out into Lake Michigan and sunk May 12, 1936

Great Lakes Marine Collection of the Milwaukee Public Library/Wisconsin Marine Historical Society

A. A. CARPENTER

OLGA 1881 — Official No. 155029

Customer – William Johnson

Plans and specifications – Wood three-masted schooner – length 137 feet – beam 30.4 feet – depth 10.0 feet – gross tons 308 – net tons 292

Final status – Abandoned at sea off Florida April 25, 1911

THOMAS H. SMITH 1881 — Official No. 145284

Customer – John Leathem and Thomas H. Smith

Plans and specifications – Wood steam barge – length 132 feet – beam 27.6 feet – depth 11.1 feet – gross tons 281 – net tons 198

Final status – Sank in collision with ARTHUR ORR in fog, 5 miles east of Racine, Wisconsin, off Wind Point, Lake Michigan November 11, 1893

Door County Maritime Museum

THOMAS H. SMITH

ALICE 1881   Official No. 105999

    Customer – William Johnson
    Plans and specifications – Wood three-masted schooner – length 137 feet – beam 30.3
        feet – depth 9.8 feet – gross tons 307 – net tons 291
    Log – Left the Lakes 1918
    Final status – Abandoned in Port Arthur, Texas 1930

Great Lakes Marine Collection of the Milwaukee Public Library/Wisconsin Marine Historical Society
ALICE

CLARA 1882   Official No. 125400

    Plans and specifications – Wood two-masted schooner – length 44.0 feet – beam 17.0 feet – depth 4.0 feet – gross tons 28.4 – net tons 27.0
    Rebuilt from schooner built in Sheboygan, Wisconsin in 1875 – gross tons 19.8

BURT BARNES 1882   Official No. 3193

    Customer – John W. Barnes
    Plans and specifications – Wood two-masted schooner – length 95.5 feet – beam 24.5 feet – depth 7.3 feet – gross tons 134 – net tons 127
    Log – Wrecked on shoal off Jackson Port, Wisconsin, Lake Michigan October 11, 1895 – raised and rebuilt in Manitowoc
    Sold Canadian 1904
    Third mast added between 1904 and 1924
    Log – Dismasted in a storm on Lake Huron 1924 – sold and repaired
    Final status – Sank off Point Petre, Lake Ontario September 2, 1926

Charles Peterson
BURT BARNES in an earlier scene with two masts.

Great Lakes Marine Collection of the Milwaukee Public Library/Wisconsin Marine Historical Society
BURT BARNES as it appeared under Canadian ownership.

J. C. PERRETT 1882   Official No. 76400

    Customer – Marinette Barge Line

    Plans and specifications – Wood steamer – length 160 feet – beam 29 feet – depth 13 feet – gross tons 537 – net tons 347

    The J. C. PERRETT transported freight by towing as many as 12 freight-laden barges at a time.

    Renamed – A. C. AMES 1895

    Final status – Abandoned and dismantled at Manitowoc, Wisconsin 1923

Great Lakes Marine Collection of the Milwaukee Public Library/Wisconsin Marine Historical Society

J. C. PERRETT

R. A. SEYMOUR JR. 1882   Official No. 110672

    Customer – John Seymour

    Rebuilt from steamer Lewis Gilbert built by Saunders, Mount Clemens, Michigan 1876 Official No. 140181

    Plans and specifications – Wood steamer – length 110 feet – beam 22.7 feet – depth 7.7 feet – gross tons 131 – net tons 103

    Engine – High pressure – non-condensing – 14.5 inch bore X 18 inch stroke – Sherriff's Manufacturing, Milwaukee, Wisconsin

    Log – Sank after striking wreck of TWO SISTERS entering the Port Washington Harbor, Port Washington, Wisconsin, Lake Michigan September 5, 1889 – re-floated and repaired.

    Final status – Abandoned 1924

Wisconsin Maritime Museum

R. A. SEYMOUR JR.

W. O. GOODMAN 1882   Official No. 80894

Plans and specifications – Wood three-masted schooner – length 144 feet – beam 30 feet – depth 10.0 feet – gross tons 324 – net tons 308

Final status – Abandoned Boston, Massachusetts 1916/17

Historical Collection of the Great Lakes, Bowling Green State University

W. O. GOODMAN

G. J. BOYCE 1884   Official No. 85850

    Customer – G. J. BOYCE
    Rebuilt from schooner Ethan Allen Official No. 7513 built by F. N. Jones in Buffalo, New York in 1857
    Plans and specifications – Wood three-masted schooner – length 137 feet – beam 30 feet – depth 10.3 feet – gross tons 319 – net tons 303
    Log – Taken to Mobile, Alabama 1916
    Final status – Stranded near Porto Padre, Cuba, Caribbean Sea January 21, 1921

Wisconsin Maritime Museum

G. J. BOYCE

Greenleaf S. Rand died December 8, 1885.

Captain Gunder Jorgensen
    Captain Gunder Jorgensen was born in Norway December 12, 1833. He immigrated to Manitowoc, Wisconsin in 1872 and married Johanne Thompson on June 1, 1863. Captain Jorgensen died on October 15, 1913.

SUCCESS 1875   Official No. 115376

    Customer – Julius Johnson
    Plans and specifications – Wood two-masted schooner – length 107 feet – beam 25.7 feet – depth 7.0 feet – gross tons 152 – net tons 144
    Final status – Wrecked Lake Michigan, 1896

TENNIE AND LAURA 1876   Official No. 145115

    Plans and specifications – Wood two-masted schooner – length 73 feet – beam 19.0 feet – depth 5.6 feet – gross tons 57 – net tons 53
    Final status – Foundered 10 miles northeast of Milwaukee, Wisconsin, Lake Michigan August 2, 1903

Great Lakes Marine Collection of the Milwaukee Public Library/Wisconsin Marine Historical Society
TENNIE AND LAURA

ISOLDA BOCK 1881   Official No. 100274

Plans and specifications – Wood two-masted schooner – length 76 feet – beam 21.5 feet – depth 6.2 feet – gross tons 70.2 – net tons 66.7
Final status – Abandoned 1925

Michigan Maritime Museum Collection
ISOLDA BOCK

Captain Francis Porter Williams
   Captain Williams was married in 1869 and died, August 5, 1893.

FARRAND H. WILLIAMS 1882   Official No. 120474
   Customer – Captain Francis P. Williams
   Plans and specifications – Wood three-masted scow schooner – length 88.9 feet
         – beam 22.8 feet – depth 6.6 feet – gross tons 94.9 – net tons 90
   Final status – Stranded Horseshoe Bay, Green Bay, Lake Michigan September 11 or
         16, 1900

Great Lakes Marine Collection of the Milwaukee Public Library/Wisconsin Marine Historical Society
FARRAND H. WILLIAMS

GRACE WILLIAMS 1885   Official No. 85882
   Customer – Captain Francis P. Williams
   Plans and specifications – Wood two-masted scow schooner – length 48.0 feet – beam
         12.2 feet – depth 5.0 feet – gross tons 22.9 – net tons 16
   Final status – Foundered off North Manitou Island, Lake Michigan May 28, 1896

Burger and Burger

Henry B. Burger acquired the balance of Rand and Burger in August of 1886 from the estate of Greenleaf S. Rand, his partner of many years. Henry B. Burger then partnered with his nephew, George B. Burger, to form Burger and Burger. George B. Burger was born October 1, 1852 in Jeffersonville, Sullivan County, New York and came to Manitowoc in 1872. Henry B. Burger died June 26, 1907.

Doris Burger Hansen

George B. Burger

RAND 1886/7   Official No. 110693

Plans and specifications – Wood steamer – length 119 feet – beam 25.6 feet – depth 9.3 feet – gross tons 191 – net tons 147
Sold Canadian – renamed SOWARDS 1909
Final status – Dismantled 1929

Historical Collection of the Great Lakes, Bowling Green State University

RAND

A. D. HAYWARD 1887   Official No. 106488

Customer – Peter D. Campbell and Mark B. Covell

Plans and specifications – Wood steamer lumber hooker – length 138 feet – beam 28.6 feet – depth 10.8 feet – gross tons 304 – net tons 224

Engine – High pressure – non-condensing – 18 inch bore X 20 inch stroke – 250 horsepower

Re-engined – Fore and aft compound – 15 inch, 30 inch bores X 28 inch stroke – 300 horsepower – Samuel F. Hodge and Company, Detroit, Michigan May 1899

Re-measured – gross tons 298 – net tons 220 April 14, 1904

Log – Blown ashore south of Harbor Beach, Michigan, Lake Huron fall 1911

Final status – Sank in a storm September 18, 1912 and went to pieces November 14, 1912

Great Lakes Marine Collection of the Milwaukee Public Library/Wisconsin Marine Historical Society

A. D. HAYWARD

EDWIN S. TICE 1887   Official No. 135954

Customer – W. D. Richards and H. C. Richards

Plans and specifications – Wood steamer lumber hooker – length 160 feet – beam 32.1 feet – depth 12.5 feet – gross 728 – net tons 578

Engine – Steeple compound – 20 inch, 38 inch bores X 36 inch stroke – 450 horsepower – Bay City Iron Works, Bay City, Michigan

Renamed – MUELLER May 6, 1901

Re-measured – length 172 feet – beam 30 feet – gross tons 699 – net tons 455 April 3, 1902

Re-measured – length 160 feet – beam 32 feet – gross tons 567 – net tons 383 1915

Final status – Dismantled Sturgeon Bay, Wisconsin September 7, 1933 – burned and sank off the stone quarry, Sturgeon Bay, Green Bay December 12, 1935

Wisconsin Maritime Museum

Launch of the EDWIN S. TICE

Great Lakes Marine Collection of the Milwaukee Public Library/Wisconsin Marine Historical Society

EDWIN S. TICE

LIZZIE METZNER 1888   Official No. 140950

    Customer – Vojta Mashek, Charles Metzner, Wenzel Seyk and Orin Vose
    Plans and specifications – Wood three-masted schooner – length 81 feet – beam 22
        feet – depth 6.8 feet – gross tons 77 – net tons 73 – cost $1200
    Sold Canadian 1904
    Final status – Wrecked east of Oswego, New York, Lake Ontario October 17, 1916

Wisconsin Maritime Museum

LIZZIE METZNER

PETOSKY 1888   Official No. 150425

    The keel of the PETOSKY was laid on Friday, it was launched on Friday and left on its maiden voyage on Friday. Each one of these circumstances was considered to be bad luck by itself, much less all three on the same vessel. Against all odds, the PETOSKY led a long and safe life.

Customer – Seymour Transportation Company
Plans and specifications – Wood freight and passenger steamer – length 171 feet
       – beam 30.4 feet – depth 12.2 feet – gross tons 771 – net tons 544
Engine – Fore and aft compound – 20 inch, 40 inch bores X 36 inch stroke – 450
       horsepower – H. G. Trout, Buffalo, New York 1888
Rebuilt – Sturgeon Bay Dry Dock Company, Sturgeon Bay, Wisconsin 1927
Final status – Burned Sturgeon Bay, Wisconsin December 3, 1935

Wisconsin Maritime Museum

Launch of the PETOSKY

Michigan Maritime Museum Collection

1888 photo of many ships in the Manitowoc River with the
PETOSKY under final construction to the far left.

Inland Seas Maritime Museum

Another 1888 view looking down the Manitowoc River with EDWIN S. TICE to the right and the Goodrich steamers CHICAGO and SHEBOYGAN to the left.

MARK B. COVELL 1888   Official No. 92006

    Customer – Campbell and Company
    Plans and specifications – Wood steamer barge – length 131 feet – beam 26.8 feet
        – depth 9.8 feet – gross 261 – net tons 246
    Engine – High pressure
    Re-engined – Steeple compound – 16 inch, 30 inch bores X 30 inch stroke – 265
        horsepower – Henry Bloeker, Grand Haven, Michigan 1890/91
    Renamed – PERE MARQUETTE #6 and rebuilt to depth of 17.4 feet – gross tons
        371 – net tons 303 1906
    Cut down to a barge in Marinette, Wisconsin and fitted with a derrick in Manitowoc,
        Wisconsin 1934
    Final status – Burned Manitowoc, Wisconsin July 5, 1936

Launch of the MARK B. COVELL

FANNIE C. HART 1888 — Official No. 120718

Customer – Hart Line C. B. and H. W. Hart
Plans and specifications – Wood freight and passenger steamer – length 143 feet – beam 30 feet – depth 10.6 feet – gross tons 398
Rebuilt with full length cabins by Burger and Burger 1889 – gross tons 476 – net tons 394
Engine – Recovered from William L. Brown – high pressure – 22 inch bore X 26 inch stroke
Re-engined – Fore and aft compound – 18 inch, 34 inch bores X 26 inch stroke – 360 horsepower – Manistee Iron Works, Manistee, Michigan 1890
Log – remodeled and renamed ROWE in New Haven, Connecticut February 15, 1912
   Sold Panamanian February 26, 1942
Final status – Scrapped in Panama 1963

FANNIE C. HART

CORA A. 1889   Official No. 126566

The CORA A. was the last commercial sailing vessel built in Manitowoc and on the Great Lakes.

Customer – Walsh and Arten

Plans and specifications – Wood three-masted schooner – length 149 feet – beam 31.5 feet – depth 11.0 feet – gross tons 381 – net tons 362 – capacity 500,000 feet of lumber

Final status – Sank 400 miles off Norfolk, Virginia, Atlantic Ocean March 6, 1916

Wisconsin Maritime Museum

Launch of the CORRA A.

Wisconsin Maritime Museum

CORA A.

CITY OF RACINE 1889   Official No. 126551

Customer – Goodrich Transportation Company
Plans and specifications – Wood freight and passenger steamer – length 204 feet – beam 40 feet – depth 13.5 feet – gross tons 1,041 – net tons 801 – cost $125,000
Engine – Fore and aft compound – 28 inch, 50 inch bores X 36 inch stroke – 1000/850 horsepower – C. F. Elmes, Chicago, Illinois
3000 people attended the launch.
Renamed ARIZONA and rebuilt Duluth, Minnesota 1909/10
Final status – Sank Maumee River, Toledo, Ohio late 1939

Great Lakes Marine Collection of the Milwaukee Public Library/Wisconsin Marine Historical Society
CITY OF RACINE

ISABELLA J. BOYCE 1889   Official No. 100446

Customer – Jonathan Boyce
Plans and specifications – Wood steamer – length 138 feet – beam 29.6 feet – depth 11.0 feet – gross 368 – net tons 317
Engine – Fore and aft compound – 19 inch, 32 inch bores X 26 inch stroke – 425 horsepower – Wilson and Hendrie, Montague, Michigan, 1889
Log – converted to a sand sucker 1915
Final status – Stranded on East Point Reef and burned off Middle Bass Island, Lake Erie June 6, 1917

Chapter 1: Early Freighters and Other Major Shipbuilding 1847 to 1951

Wisconsin Maritime Museum

Launch of the ISABELLA J. BOYCE

Inland Seas Maritime Museum

ISABELLA J. BOYCE

SIDNEY O. NEFF 1890 — Official No. 116377

Customer – Samuel Neff and Sidney O. Neff
Plans and specifications – Wood schooner – length 150 feet – beam 30 feet – depth 10.3 feet – gross tons 347 – net tons 329
Rebuilt as a propeller steamer at Milwaukee Dry Dock Company, Milwaukee, Wisconsin, 1897/98 – gross tons 436 – net tons 339
Final status – Abandoned October, 1940

CITY OF MARQUETTE 1890 — Official No. 126614

Customer – Emil G. Richards and Charles W. Endress
Plans and specifications – Wood freight and passenger steamer – length 114 feet – beam 25.3 feet – depth 9.1 feet – gross tons 341 – net tons 295
Engine – High pressure from steamer ST. MARIES
Re-engined – Fore and aft compound – 15 inch, 30 inch bores X 24 inch stroke – 300 horsepower – S. F. Hodge Company, Detroit, Michigan, 1895
Converted to a barge – gross tons 171 Escanaba, Michigan, 1930
Renamed – ACHING HEARTS and used as a cement barge
Final status – Rolled over and sank Mackinaw City Michigan – raised and sunk at New Shoal Number 3, Straits of Mackinaw, Mackinaw City, Michigan early 1930s

Inland Seas Maritime Museum

CITY OF MARQUETTE

INDIANA 1890 — Official No. 100471

Customer – Goodrich Transportation Company
Plans and specifications – Wood freight and passenger steamer – length 201 feet – beam 35.4 feet – depth 14.3 feet – gross 1,177 – net tons 962 – cost $135,000
Engine – Fore and aft compound – 26 inch, 50 inch bores X 36 inch stroke – 775 horsepower – C. F. Elmes, Chicago, Illinois
Rebuilt – Manitowoc Shipbuilding Company, Manitowoc, Wisconsin – lengthened 22 feet, steel bulkheads added, new boiler – gross tons 1979 1915/16
Final status – Sank Maumee River, Toledo, Ohio, abandoned December 1937

Chapter 1: Early Freighters and Other Major Shipbuilding 1847 to 1951

Great Lakes Marine Collection of the Milwaukee Public Library/Wisconsin Marine Historical Society

Hull construction on the INDIANA with a derrick along side
and the boiler on cribs aft, still outside of the hull

Great Lakes Marine Collection of the Milwaukee Public Library/Wisconsin Marine Historical Society

Launch of the INDIANA

Inland Seas Maritime Museum

The INDIANA was the flagship of the Goodrich Transportation Company in 1891.

EUGENE C. HART 1890   Official No. 136131

Customer – Hart Line C. B. and H. W. Hart

Plans and specifications – Wood freight and passenger steamer – length 127 feet – beam 25.0 feet – depth 9.5 feet – gross 407 – net tons 361

Engine – High pressure – non-condensing – 22 inch bore X 27 inch stroke – 280 horsepower

Rebuilt – length 153 feet – beam 25.0 feet – depth 9.4 feet – gross tons 522 – net tons 478 1892/93

Re-engined – Fore and aft compound – 16 inch, 36 inch bores X 30 inch stroke – 425 horsepower – Montague Iron Works, Montague, Michigan 1902

Log – renamed NORLAND, April 2, 1919

Final status – Foundered 8 miles off St. Francis south of Milwaukee, Wisconsin, Lake Michigan November 13, 1922.

Inland Seas Maritime Museum

EUGENE C. HART

EDWARD BUCKLEY 1891   Official No. 136252
> Customer – Edward Buckley, Captain Charles Gnewuch and William Nuttall
> Plans and specifications – Wood steamer lumber hooker – length 154 feet – beam 31.7 feet – depth 10.6 feet – gross 414 – net tons 313
> Engine – Fore and aft compound – 18 inch, 36 inch bores X 30 inch stroke – 600 horsepower – Wilson and Hendrie, Montague, Michigan 1891
> Sold Canadian May, 1922
> Final status – Burned near Picnic Island, North Channel, Lake Huron September 4, 1929

Wisconsin Maritime Museum

EDWARD BUCKLEY loaded with timber locking through at Sault St. Marie, Michigan.

MYRTLE CAMP 1892   Official No. 92416
> Customer – C. O. Thompson
> Plans and specifications – Wood two-masted schooner – length 68 feet – beam 18.1 feet – depth 5.6 feet – gross tons 49 – net tons 46
> Final status – last record 1911

LOTUS 1893/94   Official No. 141298
> Customer – J. B. Moran
> Plans and specifications – Wood steamer – length 111 feet – beam 22.0 feet – depth 8.7 feet – gross tons 219 – net tons 188
> Engine – Fore and aft compound – 16 inch, 30 inch bores X 24 inch stroke – 550 horsepower – Wilson and Hendrie, Montague, Michigan 1893
> Rebuilt into a tug Grand Haven, Michigan January 1933

Great Lakes Marine Collection of the Milwaukee Public Library/Wisconsin Marine Historical Society

LOTUS

Manitowoc County Historical Society, INC

The 1870 dry dock shown in 1895 as part of the Burger and Burger yard.

In 1895 a breakwater extension, that ran southeast/northwest, was built off the existing north pier. At the same time, the south pier was extended 500 feet and the inner end was shortened by 320 feet with 2000 feet of piling driven to the south to make the first carferry dock.

IOWA 1896   Official No. 100613

Customer – Goodrich Transportation Company
Plans and specifications – Wood freight and passenger steamer – length 203 feet – beam 36.4 feet – depth 13 feet – gross tons 1,157 – net tons 846 – cost $145,000
Built from the steamer MENOMINEE
Engine – Steeple compound – 21 inch, 42 inch bores X 36 inch stroke – 950 horsepower – C. F. Elmes, Chicago, Illinois
Rebuilt – upper deck covered and added lifeboats
Log – Rammed by the SHEBOYGAN in the Chicago River, July 17, 1913 and sank – raised and repaired
Final status – Crushed by ice and sank 3 miles off Chicago, Illinois, Lake Michigan February 4, 1915

Inland Seas Maritime Museum

IOWA completing rebuild from the MENOMENEE

Great Lakes Marine Collection of the Milwaukee Public Library/Wisconsin Marine Historical Society

IOWA with a big load of excursionists

The Manitowoc harbor was dredged to a depth of 20 feet from Lake Michigan up the Manitowoc River for 5500 feet, with a turning basin at the end, adjacent to the Burger and Burger yard, circa 1897.

<u>GEORGIA 1898</u>   <u>Official No. 125873</u>

    Customer – Goodrich Transit Company
    Plans and specifications – Wood freight and passenger steamer – length 196 feet –
        beam 34.4 feet – depth 12.0 feet – gross 895 – net tons 811 – cost $120,000
    Built from the steamer CITY OF LUDINGTON
    Engine – Fore and aft compound – 21 inch, 44 inch bores X 36 inch stroke – Dry
        Dock Engine Works, Detroit, Michigan 1898
    Log – Re-boilered and overhauled 1914
        Sank Manitowoc River February 19, 1920 – raised and refurbished
        Laid up Sturgeon Bay, Wisconsin 1926/7 – dismantled
    Final status – Hull towed to Big Summer Island, Green Bay, Lake
        Michigan and sunk to form a dock during the summer or fall of 1932

Inland Seas Maritime Museum

GEORGIA

In 1900/01, the Manitowoc River was dredged to a depth of 20 feet from the turning basin around Lueps Peninsula to provide room for more vessels.

Manitowoc Dry Dock Company

    Elias Gunnel was born in Ardee, north of Dublin, Ireland on March 13, 1866 and immigrated to America in 1875 to Rochester, New York, then on to Buffalo, New York. He apprenticed at the Union Dry Dock Company then served as superintendant at numerous yards until moving to the Chicago Shipbuilding Company in 1892. Ellias Gunnel worked at the Chicago Shipbuilding Company as Plant Superintendent. At the same time, Charles C. West was a mechanical engineer for the Chicago Shipbuilding Company. He was born in Chicago, Illinois on September 22, 1878, and graduated from Cornell University with a degree in mechanical engineering in 1900. In 1899, Chicago Shipbuilding was absorbed by a merger into American Shipbuilding Company, effectively taking away control over the yard's destiny. Seeing little future at Chicago Shipbuilding, the two men wanted to strike out on their own. After considering starting their own new yard, they were advised by others in the shipping business to buy an established yard and specifically to look at Burger and Burger. Henry B. Burger, principle owner, and his partner

George B. Burger, were looking to retire. So Gunnell and West along with Lynford E. Geer, an accountant, also from Chicago Shipbuilding, and Thomas J. Prindeville, an insurance broker, formed Manitowoc Dry Dock Company on June 27, 1902 to purchase Burger and Burger. Company officers were: Ellias Gunnel – President; Thomas J. Prindeville – Vice President; Lynford E. Geer – Secretary/Treasurer; and Charles C. West – General Manager. Financing for the purchase was arranged based on bringing steel shipbuilding technology from the Chicago yard to the otherwise capable and busy Burger and Burger yard. The transfer of operation of the yards was completed on October 11, 1902. In August of 1902, Elias Gunnell took leave to demonstrate pneumatic tools in Europe, so George B. Burger stayed on as plant superintendent to see the new company through the transition as well as provide his expertise in wood vessel repair. Transfer of ownership was completed on August 13, 1903. Since Burger and Burger was engaged in building and repairing wood vessels, a long term program was started to re-equip the yard to build and repair steel ships. There were 90 employees at the time.

The Manitowoc Company, Inc
Charles C. West.

The Manitowoc Company, Inc
Elias Gunnell

CHEQUAMEGON 1903 Hull #1   Official No. 127764
    Construction started under Burger and Burger and was completed under Manitowoc
        Dry Dock Company.
    Customer – Chequamegon Bay Transport Company
    Plans and specifications – Wood freight and passenger steamer – length 101 feet
        – beam 22 feet – depth 9.5 feet – gross tons 141 – net tons 112
    Engine – Triple expansion – 12 inch, 19 inch, 32 inch bores X 20 inch stroke – 500
        horsepower – Montague Iron Works, Montague, Michigan
    Renamed PERE MARQUETTE #7 1911
    Converted to a tug – renamed Robert C. Pringle 1918
    Final status – Foundered 15 miles southeast of Manitowoc, Wisconsin, Lake
        Michigan June 20, 1922

Wisconsin Maritime Museum

Launch of the CHEQUAMEGON

Wisconsin Maritime Museum

CHEQUAMEGON

In 1904, a separate business called the Gunnell Tool Company was created by Gunnell, West, and Geer to build pneumatic riveting equipment used for among other things, steel shipbuilding. In 1905, a new large plant was built and the name was changed to the Gunnell Machine Company.

MAYWOOD 1905 Hull #6　　　　　　　　　　　　　　　Official no. 202202

　　Customer – Escanaba and Gladstone Transportation Company – James B. Moran
　　Plans and specifications – Steel freight and passenger steamer – length 130 feet
　　　　– beam 28 feet – depth 17 feet – gross tons 398 – net tons 309
　　Engine – Triple Expansion – 14 inch, 22 inch, 36 inch bores X 24 inch stroke – 700
　　　　horsepower – Marine Iron Works, Chicago, Illinois
　　Sold – French – renamed INCA July 16, 1917
　　Final status – unknown after 1934

Wisconsin Maritime Museum

MAYWOOD

In May 1908, Manitowoc Dry Dock Company purchased Manitowoc Steam Boiler Works giving the yard the direct ability to repair, replace or install new boilers in ships.

UNITED STATES 1909 Hull #28   Official No. 206330

Customer – Indiana Transportation Company

Plans and specifications – Steel freight and passenger steamer – length 204 feet – beam 41 feet – depth 16 feet – gross tons 1,711 – net tons 1,040

Engine – Triple compound – 22 inch, 36.5 inch, 60 inch bores X 40 inch stroke – 2,650 horsepower – Gunnell Machine Company, Manitowoc, Wisconsin 1908

Log – Lengthened to 258 feet – gross tons 2,064 and converted to a yacht New York, New York December 1916/17

Burned in Sarnia, Ontario, Canada March 5, 1928 – rebuilt to a freighter at Lauzon, Quebec, Canada 1929

Renamed BASTICAN May 1930

Final status – Scrapped in Sorel, Quebec, Canada December 1945

Wisconsin Maritime Museum

Launch of the UNITED STATES

In 1909, the Gunnell Machine Company was merged into the Manitowoc Dry Dock Company.

ALABAMA 1910 Hull #36   Official No. 207138

    Customer – Goodrich Transit Company
    Plans and specifications – Steel freight and passenger steamer – length 272 feet – beam 45.5 feet – depth 26.1 feet – gross tons 2,626 – net tons 1,684 – cost $386,000
    Engine – Triple expansion – 23 inch, 38 inch, 62 inch bores X 36 inch stroke – 2,000 horsepower – Toledo Shipbuilding Company, Toledo, Ohio
    Cut down to a barge in Holland, Michigan 1963 and 1964 for Stender Marine Corporation Bay City, Michigan
    Current status – Scrap metal barge Detroit, Michigan

Great Lakes Marine Collection of the Milwaukee Public Library/Wisconsin Marine Historical Society

ALABAMA under construction with the launch ways in place

Wisconsin Maritime Museum

Launch of the ALABAMA

Wisconsin Maritime Museum

ALABAMA

The company's name was changed to the Manitowoc Ship Building and Dry Dock Company in 1910. From 1910 through 1912, the company built six sections of floating dry dock making up to 360 feet in length. George B. Burger died June 27, 1911.

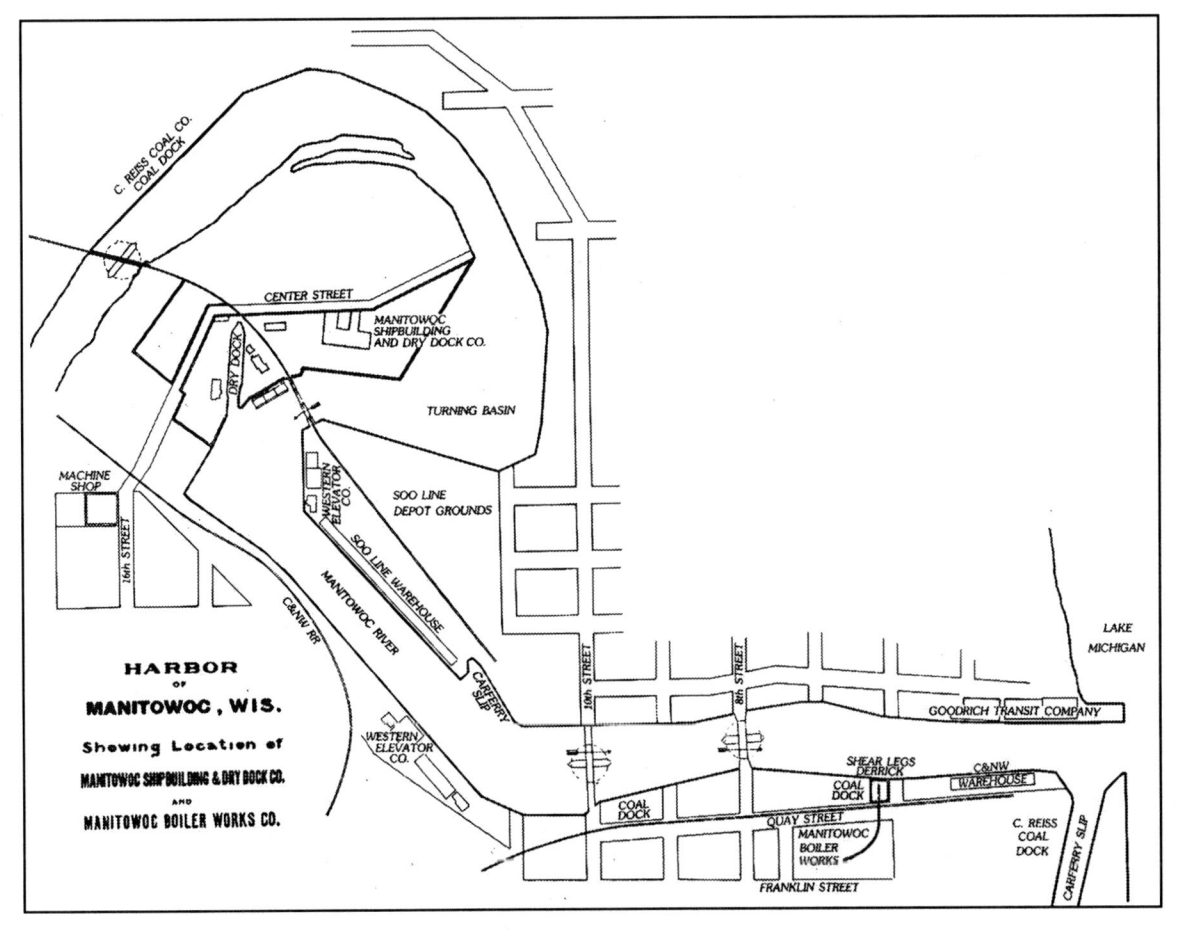

Map of Manitowoc, circa 1911

View of the Manitowoc Shipbuilding and Dry Dock Company yard with
a ship being lengthened in the 1870 graving yard around 1911.

<u>NEVADA 1915 Hull #70</u> <u>Official No. 213782</u>

    Customer – Goodrich Transit Company
    Plans and specifications – Steel freight and passenger steamer – length 221 feet – beam
        42.2 feet – depth 24.7 feet – gross tons 2,122 – net tons 1,078 – cost $411,000
    Engine – Triple expansion – 22 inch, 35 inch, 56 inch bores X 36 inch stroke – 1,600
        horsepower – Great Lakes Engineering Works, Detroit, Michigan
    Sold Russian – Renamed ROGDAY 1917
    Log – Returned to the United States – renamed NEVADA 1921
        – Rebuilt as a freighter 1935
    Final status – Foundered off South Carolina coast, Atlantic Ocean December 16, 1943

Manitowoc County Historical Society, INC

NEVADA

Chapter 1: Early Freighters and Other Major Shipbuilding 1847 to 1951   93

The company's name was shortened to the Manitowoc Shipbuilding Company in 1916. The Manitowoc Steam Boiler Works was merged into the Manitowoc Shipbuilding Company.

Thirty-eight Lakers were built to transport military support equipment and materials to the theaters of World War I. Employment rose to around 2,700 for this effort.

LAKE ONEIDA 1917 Hull #80   Official No. US 215630

    Started as ADA

    Customer – BergHansen US Shipping Board Emergency Fleet Corporation
    Plans and specifications – Steel freighter – length 259 feet – beam 43.5 feet – depth 23.1 feet – gross tons 2,063 – net tons 1,434
    Engine – Diesel
    Remeasured – gross tons 2,124 – net tons 1,667 1921
    Final status – Stranded Terminal Island San Pedro Harbor, California December 27, 1936

Wisconsin Maritime Museum

ADA that became the LAKE ONEIDA

LAKE MOHAWK 1917 Hull #81   Official No. US 215702

    Started as MOTOR 1

    Customer – BergHansen US Shipping Board Emergency Fleet Corporation
    Plans and specifications – Steel freighter – length 250 feet – beam 43.5 feet – depth 23.1 feet – gross tons 2,124 – net tons 1,667
    Engine – Diesel
    Final status – Torpedoed and sank off Cape Hatteras, North Carolina, Atlantic Ocean July 15, 1942

LAKE ONTARIO 1917 Hull #82   Official No. US 215816

    Started as WAR CASTLE

    Customer – C. Hannevig US Shipping Board Emergency Fleet Corporation
    Plans and specifications – Steel freighter – length 251 feet – beam 43.5 feet – depth 23.1 feet – gross tons 2,003 – net tons 1,211
    Engine – Triple expansion – 20 inch, 33 inch, 54 inch bores X 40 inch stroke – 1,250 horsepower
    Final status – Scrapped Ford Dearborn, Michigan 1928

LAKE VIEW 1917 Hull #83 — Official No. US 215773
Started as WAR VICTOR

Customer – C. Hannevig US Shipping Board Emergency Fleet Corporation
Plans and specifications – Steel freighter – length 251 feet – beam 43.5 feet – depth 23.1 feet – gross tons 2,003 – net tons 1,211
Engine – Triple expansion – 20 inch, 33 inch, 54 inch bores X 40 inch stroke – 1,250 horsepower
Final status – Scrapped Ford Dearborn, Michigan 1928

LAKE PEWAUKEE 1918 Hull #86 — Official No. US 216226
Started as WAR SENTRY

Customer – US Shipping Board Emergency Fleet Corporation
Plans and specifications – Steel freighter – length 251 feet – beam 43.5 feet – depth 23.1 feet – gross ton 2,177 – net tons 1,284
Engine – Triple expansion – 20 inch, 33 inch, 54 inch bores X 40 inch stroke – 1,250 horsepower
Final status – Scrapped Ford Dearborn, Michigan 1928

LAKE SHAWANO 1918 Hull #87 — Official No. US 216278

Customer – C. Hannevig US Shipping Board Emergency Fleet Corporation
Plans and specifications – Steel freighter – length 251 feet – beam 43.5 feet – depth 23.1 feet – gross tons 2,177 – net tons 1,287
Engine – Triple expansion – 20 inch, 33 inch, 54 inch bores X 40 inch stroke – 1,250 horsepower
Final status – Scrapped Ford Dearborn, Michigan 1933

LAKE LIDA 1918 Hull #88 — Official No. US 216277

Customer – C. Hannevig US Shipping Board Emergency Fleet Corporation
Plans and specifications – Steel freighter – length 251 feet – beam 43.5 feet – depth 23.1 feet – gross tons 2,177 – net tons 1,287
Engine – Triple expansion – 20 inch, 33 inch, 54 inch bores X 40 inch stroke – 1,250 horsepower
Final status – Scrapped Ford Dearborn, Michigan 1928

LAKE MONROE 1918 Hull #90 — Official No. US 216739
Started as WAR COMET

Customer – Cunard Line US Shipping Board Emergency Fleet Corporation
Plans and specifications – Steel freighter – length 251 feet – beam 43.5 feet – depth 23.1 feet – gross tons 2,150 – net tons 1,286
Engine – Triple expansion – 20 inch, 33 inch, 54 inch bores X 40 inch stroke – 1,250 horsepower
Final status – Scuttled Atlantic Ocean September 5, 1947

LAKE GREENWOOD 1918 Hull #91   Official No. US 216616

    Started as WAR MIST

    Customer – Cunard Line US Shipping Board Emergency Fleet Corporation
    Plans and specifications – Steel freighter – length 250 feet – beam 43.5 feet – depth 23.1 feet – gross tons 2,150 – net tons 1,286
    Engine – Triple expansion – 20 inch, 33 inch, 54 inch bores X 40 inch stroke – 1,250 horsepower
    Final status – Scrapped LaSpezia, Italy 1956

LAKE ANNETTE 1918 Hull #92   Official No. US 216403

    Customer – R. Lawrence Smith US Shipping Board Emergency Fleet Corporation
    Plans and specifications – Steel freighter – length 251 feet – beam 43.5 feet – depth 23.1 feet – gross tons 2,177 – net tons 1,287
    Engine – Triple expansion – 20 inch, 33 inch, 54 inch bores X 40 inch stroke – 1,250 horsepower
    Final status – Scrapped Ford Dearborn, Michigan 1928

LAKE LINDEN 1918 Hull #93   Official No. US 216805

    Customer – Cunard Line US Shipping Board Emergency Fleet Corporation
    Plans and specifications – Steel freighter – length 251 feet – beam 43.5 feet – depth 23.1 feet – gross tons 2,150 – net tons 1,286
    Engine – Triple expansion – 20 inch, 33 inch, 54 inch bores X 40 inch stroke – 1,200 horsepower
    Final status – Scrapped Ford Dearborn, Michigan 1927

LAKE WINTHROP 1918 Hull #94   Official No. US 216780

    Started as WAR METEOR

    Customer – Cunard Line US Shipping Board Emergency Fleet Corporation
    Plans and specifications – Steel freighter – length 251 feet – beam 43.5 feet – depth 23.1 feet – gross tons 2,150 – net tons 1,286
    Engine – Triple expansion – 20 inch, 33 inch, 54 inch bores X 40 inch stroke – 1,250 horsepower
    Final status – Stranded south of Rorvik, Norway September 16, 1931 – raised – scrapped Stavanger, Norway 1932

LAKE WILSON 1918 Hull #95   Official No. US 216959

    Started as WAR SKY

    Customer – Cunard Line US Shipping Board Emergency Fleet Corporation
    Plans and specifications – Steel freighter – length 251 feet – beam 43.5 feet – depth 23.1 feet – gross tons 2,139 – net tons 1,275
    Engine – Triple expansion – 20 inch, 33 inch, 54 inch bores X 40 inch stroke – 1,550 horsepower
    Final status – Scrapped Ford Dearborn, Michigan 1928

LAKE KYTTLE 1918 Hull #96 — Official No. US 217087

Customer – US Shipping Board Emergency Fleet Corporation

Plans and specifications – Steel freighter – length 251 feet – beam 43.5 feet – depth 23.1 feet – gross tons 2,157 – net tons 1,285

Engine – Triple expansion – 20 inch, 33 inch, 54 inch bores X 40 inch stroke – 1,400 horsepower

Final status – Foundered off Saybrook, Connecticut, Long Island Sound, Atlantic Ocean January 20, 1960

CORRALES 1918 Hull #97 — Official No. US 217197

Customer – US Shipping Board Emergency Fleet Corporation

Plans and specifications – Steel freighter – length 251 feet – beam 43.5 feet – depth 23.1 feet – gross tons 2,146 – net tons 1,285

Engine – Triple expansion – 20 inch, 33 inch, 54 inch bores X 40 inch stroke – 1,250 horsepower

Final status – Beached with leaks Pimentol, Peru, Pacific Ocean August 10, 1964

CORSICANA 1918 Hull #98 — Official No. US 217011

Customer – US Shipping Board Emergency Fleet Corporation

Plans and specifications – Steel freighter – length 251 feet – beam 43.5 feet – depth 23.1 feet – gross tons 2,146 – net tons 1,285

Engine – Triple expansion – 20 inch, 33 inch, 54 inch bores X 40 inch stroke – 1,200 horsepower

Final status – Scrapped Hong Kong June, 1962

View of Manitowoc Shipbuilding Company in 1918 showing many Lakers under construction.

COPRES 1919 Hull #99   Official No. US 217585

    Customer – Saginaw Dock and Terminal Company, US Shipping Board Emergency Fleet Corporation
    Plans and specifications – Steel freighter – length 251 feet – beam 43.5 feet – depth 23.1 feet – gross tons 2,153 – net tons 1,280
    Engine – Triple expansion – 20 inch, 33 inch, 54 inch bores X 40 inch stroke – 1,250 horsepower
    Renamed Aetna 1926
    Renamed Saginaw 1937
    Final status – Scrapped Finland June, 1967

Wisconsin Maritime Museum

COPRES

COQUINA 1919 Hull #100   Official No. US 217871

    Customer – US Shipping Board Emergency Fleet Corporation
    Plans and specifications – Steel freighter – length 251 feet – beam 43.5 feet – depth 23.1 feet – gross tons 2,153 – net tons 1,280
    Engine – Triple expansion – 20 inch, 33 inch, 54 inch bores X 40 inch stroke – 1,200 horsepower
    Final status – Sank Pacific Ocean December 7, 1941

CORAPEAK 1919 Hull #101   Official No. US 217850

    Customer – US Shipping Board Emergency Fleet Corporation
    Plans and specifications – Steel freighter – length 251 feet – beam 43.5 feet – depth 23.1 feet – gross tons 2,153 – net tons 1,280
    Engine – Triple expansion – 20 inch, 33 inch, 54 inch bores X 40 inch stroke – 1,250 horsepower
    Renamed CASTILLA in Chile 1940
    Final status – Foundered South Atlantic Ocean December 11, 1954

CORCORAN 1919 Hull #102   Official No. US 218058

    Customer – US Shipping Board Emergency Fleet Corporation
    Plans and specifications – Steel freighter – length 251 feet – beam 43.5 feet – depth 23.1 feet – gross tons 2,153 – net tons 1,280
    Engine – Triple expansion – 20 inch, 33 inch, 54 inch bores X 40 inch stroke – 1,250 horsepower
    Renamed CARRYALL and cut down to a barge 1936
    Final status – Out of documentation 1963

PYTHON 1919 Hull #103   Official No. US 217954

    Started as CORNING

    Customer – US Shipping Board Emergency Fleet Corporation
    Plans and specifications – Steel freighter – length 251 feet – beam 43.5 feet – depth 23.1 feet – gross tons 2,153 – net tons 1,280
    Engine – Triple expansion – 20 inch, 33 inch, 54 inch bores X 40 inch stroke – 1,250 horsepower
    Renamed BRUNSWICK 1926
    Renamed SUMIDA MARU 1926
    Final status – Sank 75 miles southeast of Mauroran Hokkaido Island, Japan, Pacific Ocean April 15, 1944

CORNUCOPIA 1919 Hull #104   Official No. US 218057

    Customer – US Shipping Board Emergency Fleet Corporation
    Plans and specifications – Steel freighter – length 251 feet – beam 43.5 feet – depth 23.1 feet – gross tons 2,153 – net tons 1,280
    Engine – Triple expansion – 20 inch, 33 inch, 54 inch bores X 40 inch stroke – 1,250 horsepower
    Renamed BELIZE in Norway 1937
    Final status – Missing in the Atlantic Ocean off St. John, New Brunswick December 4, 1941

LAKE GADSDEN 1919 Hull #105   Official No. US 218718

    Customer – US Shipping Board Emergency Fleet Corporation
    Plans and specifications – Steel freighter – length 253 feet – beam 43.8 feet – depth 26.2 feet – gross tons 2,689 – net tons 1,672
    Engine – Triple expansion – 20 inch, 33 inch, 54 inch bores X 40 inch stroke – 1,250 horsepower
    Sold Panamanian 1947
    Final status – Stranded and sank near Cabo Corrubedo light off the coast of Spain July 16, 1954

LAKE ONAWA 1919 Hull #106   Official No. US 219100

    Customer – US Shipping Board Emergency Fleet Corporation
    Plans and specifications – Steel freighter – length 254 feet – beam 43.9 feet – depth 25.9 feet – gross tons 2,711 – net tons 1,672
    Engine – Triple expansion – 20 inch, 33 inch, 54 inch bores X 40 inch stroke – 1,250 horsepower
    Renamed SINSEI MARU NO. 5 in Japan 1936
    Final status – Lost off San Isidro, Philippine Islands, Pacific Ocean December 7, 1944

LAKE SAVUS 1919 Hull #107   Official No. US 218922

Customer – US Shipping Board Emergency Fleet Corporation

Plans and specifications – Steel freighter – length 253 feet – beam 43.8 feet – depth 26.2 feet – gross tons 2,689 – net tons 1,660

Engine – Triple expansion – 20 inch, 33 inch, 54 inch bores X 40 inch stroke – 1,250 horsepower

Final status – Scrapped Kaohsiung, Formosa 1959

LAKE GAITHER 1919 Hull #108   Official No. US 219121

Customer – US Shipping Board Emergency Fleet Corporation

Plans and specifications – Steel freighter – length 253 feet – beam 43.8 feet – depth 26.2 feet – gross tons 2,689 – net tons 1,672

Engine – Triple expansion – 20 inch, 33 inch, 54 inch bores X 40 inch stroke – 1,500 horsepower

Sold British 1941

Final status – Scrapped in Turkey 1968

LAKE GALATA 1919 Hull #109   Official No. US 219090

Customer – US Shipping Board Emergency Fleet Corporation

Plans and specifications – Steel freighter – length 253 feet – beam 43.8 feet – depth 26.2 feet – gross tons 2,689 – net tons 1,672

Engine – Triple expansion – 20 inch, 33 inch, 54 inch bores X 40 inch stroke – 1,500 horsepower

Final status – Torpedoed by German submarine – sank northeast of Cape Samana Santo Domingo, Caribbean Sea July 3, 1942

LAKE GALEWOOD 1919 Hull #110   Official No. US 219120

Customer – US Shipping Board Emergency Fleet Corporation

Plans and specifications – Steel freighter – length 253 feet – beam 43.8 feet – depth 26.2 feet – gross tons 2,689 – net tons 1,672

Engine – Triple expansion – 20 inch, 33 inch, 54 inch bores X 40 inch stroke – 1,500 horsepower

Final status – Burned and sank near the Aleutian Islands, Pacific Ocean December 23, 1943

LAKE GALIEN 1919 Hull #111   Official No. US 219118

Customer – US Shipping Board Emergency Fleet Corporation

Plans and specifications – Steel freighter – length 253 feet – beam 43.8 feet – depth 26.2 feet – gross tons 2,689 – net tons 1,672

Engine – Triple expansion – 20 inch, 33 inch, 54 inch bores X 40 inch stroke – 1,500 horsepower

Final status – Sank North Atlantic Ocean June 1, 1942

LAKE GALISTEO 1919 Hull #112   Official No. US 219701

Customer – US Shipping Board Emergency Fleet Corporation

Plans and specifications – Steel freighter – length 253 feet – beam 43.8 feet – depth 26.2 feet – gross tons 2,689 – net tons 1,672

Engine – Triple expansion – 20 inch, 33 inch, 54 inch bores X 40 inch stroke – 1,500 horsepower

Renamed HAI DEAN in China 1946

Final status – Scrapped Formosa 1954

LAKE IKATAN 1920 Hull #113   Official No. US 219593

Customer – US Shipping Board Emergency Fleet Corporation
Plans and specifications – Steel freighter – length 253 feet – beam 43.8 feet – depth 26.2 feet – gross tons 2,689 – net tons 1,672
Engine – Triple expansion – 20 inch, 33 inch, 54 inch bores X 40 inch stroke – 1,100 horsepower
Renamed HAI MING and HAI LIAO in China 1946
Log – in service 1968
Final status – Dropped from registry between 1969 and 1972

RIPON 1920 Hull #114   Official No. US 219702

Started as LAKE GALVA

Customer – US Shipping Board Emergency Fleet Corporation
Plans and specifications – Steel freighter – length 253 feet – beam 43.8 feet – depth 26.2 feet – gross tons 2,689 – net tons 1,672
Engine – Triple expansion – 20 inch, 33 inch, 54 inch bores X 40 inch stroke – 1,200 horsepower
Sold Russian and renamed INDIGIRKA 1938
Last known status – In service 1950

WAUWATOSA 1920 Hull #115   Official No. US 219591

Started as LAKE IDRIA

Customer – US Shipping Board Emergency Fleet Corporation
Plans and specifications – Steel freighter – length 253 feet – beam 43.8 feet – depth 26.2 feet – gross tons 2,689 – net tons 1,667
Engine – Triple expansion – 20 inch, 33 inch, 54 inch bores X 40 inch stroke – 1,500 horsepower
Final status – Abandoned and scrapped Boston, Massachusetts 1929

SIOUX CITY 1920 Hull #116   Official No. US 219700

Started as LAKE GAMA

Customer – US Shipping Board Emergency Fleet Corporation
Plans and specifications – Steel freighter – length 253 feet – beam 43.8 feet – depth 26.2 feet – gross tons 2,689 – net tons 1,667
Engine – Triple expansion – 20 inch, 33 inch, 54 inch bores X 40 inch stroke – 1,500 horsepower
Renamed ORTEGO 1924
Log – Stranded and abandoned near Jeremie, Haiti Caribbean Sea November 12, 1928
Final status – Scrapped Jacksonville, Florida 1929

LAKE HARESTI 1920 Hull #117   Official No. US 219703

Customer – US Shipping Board Emergency Fleet Corporation
Plans and specifications – Steel freighter – length 253 feet – beam 43.8 feet – depth 26.2 feet – gross tons 2,689 – net tons 1,667
Engine – Triple expansion – 20 inch, 33 inch, 54 inch bores X 40 inch stroke – 1,500 horsepower
Sold Russian and renamed SHCHORS 1938
Last known status – Not reported after 1950

Wisconsin Maritime Museum

Launch of the LAKE HARESTI

LAKE HORUS 1920 Hull #118

Launched, not completed, contract cancelled

Customer – US Shipping Board Emergency Fleet Corporation

Plans and specifications – Steel freighter – length 253 feet – beam 43.8 feet – depth 26.2 feet – gross tons 2,689 – net tons 1,667

Engine – Triple expansion – 20 inch, 33 inch, 54 inch bores X 40 inch stroke – 1,500 horsepower

LAKE HYAS 1920 Hull #119

Not built, contract cancelled

Customer – US Shipping Board Emergency Fleet Corporation

Plans and specifications – Steel freighter – length 253 feet – beam 43.8 feet – depth 26.2 feet – gross tons 2,689 – net tons 1,667

Engine – Triple expansion – 20 inch, 33 inch, 54 inch bores X 40 inch stroke – 1,500 horsepower

LAKE HYBLA 1920 Hull #120

Not built, contract cancelled

Customer – US Shipping Board Emergency Fleet Corporation

Plans and specifications – Steel freighter – length 253 feet – beam 43.8 feet – depth 26.2 feet – gross tons 2,689 – net tons 1,667

Engine – Triple expansion – 20 inch, 33 inch, 54 inch bores X 40 inch stroke – 1,500 horsepower

LAKE HYGEIA 1920 Hull #121

Not built, contract cancelled

Customer – US Shipping Board Emergency Fleet Corporation

Plans and specifications – Steel freighter – length 253 feet – beam 43.8 feet – depth 26.2 feet – gross tons 2,689 – net tons 1,667

Engine – Triple expansion – 20 inch, 33 inch, 54 inch bores X 40 inch stroke – 1,500 horsepower

LAKE HYPANIA 1920 Hull #122

Not built, contract cancelled

Customer – US Shipping Board Emergency Fleet Corporation

Plans and specifications – Steel freighter – length 253 feet – beam 43.8 feet – depth 26.2 feet – gross tons 2,689 – net tons 1,667

Engine – Triple expansion – 20 inch, 33 inch, 54 inch bores X 40 inch stroke – 1,500 horsepower

CAYO MAMBI 1920 Hull #123   Official No. US 220287

Customer – Atlantic Fruit Company

Plans and specifications – Steel freighter – length 250 feet – beam 37.7 feet – depth 14.8 feet – gross tons 1,925 – net tons 1,055

Engine – 2,000 horsepower

Last known status – In service 1966

CANANOVA 1920 Hull #124   Official No. US 220388

Customer – Atlantic Fruit Company

Plans and specifications – Steel freighter – length 250 feet – beam 37.7 feet – depth 14.8 feet – gross tons 1,925 – net tons 1055

Engine – 1,900 horsepower

Sold Russian and renamed PETROPAVLOSK 1939

Last known status – Unknown after 1958

Wisconsin Maritime Museum

CANANOVA

The company's name was changed to the Manitowoc Shipbuilding Corporation in 1920. Elias Gunnell retired and was succeeded as president by Charles C. West in 1920.

JOHN A. KLING 1922 Hull #204   Official No. 222512

    Customer – Reiss Steamship Company
    Plans and specifications – Steel self-unloading steamer – length 438 feet – beam 56.2 feet – depth 28.4 feet – gross tons 5,412 – net tons 4,003
    Engine – Triple expansion – 21 inch, 35 inch, 42 inch X 42 inch stroke – 1500 horsepower
    Lengthened – 561 feet – gross tons 6,825 – net tons 5,417 – Manitowoc Shipbuilding, Manitowoc, Wisconsin 1940
    Re-engined and rebuilt – diesel – 12 cylinder – 15.5 inch bore X 22 inch stroke – 3,400 horsepower – Cooper Bessemer – controllable pitch propeller – new deck house, pilot house and bow thruster – Christy Corporation, Sturgeon Bay, Wisconsin 1965/66
    Renamed LEADALE 1981
    Log – Grounded and sank Thorold, Ontario December 7, 1982 – raised and towed to Humberstone Ontario, Canada
    Final status – Scrapped 1983

Wisconsin Maritime Museum

JOHN A. KLING hull nearing completion

Wisconsin Maritime Museum

The JOHN A. KLING was the first of the modern bulk freighters built in Manitowoc.

Wisconsin Maritime Museum

JOHN A. KLING in the floating dry dock

The company built the seventh section of the floating steel dry dock in 1923.

PERE MARQUETTE 21 1924 Hull #209 Official No. 223796

The PERE MARQUETTE 21 was the first cross-lake carferry built in Manitowoc.

Customer – Pere Marquette Railway Company
Plans and specifications – Steel carferry steamer – length 360 feet – beam 56 feet
 – depth 19.5 feet – gross tons 2,985 – net tons – 1,511 – capacity four tracks,
 30 railroad cars – cost $800,000 – service speed 15 miles per hour
Engines – Two triple expansion – 20.5 inch, 34 inch, 56 inch bores X 36 inch stroke
 – 2,700 horsepower
Re-engined – Two Steeple compound – Unaflow – 19.5 inch, 43 inch bores X 46 inch
 stroke – Skinner Engine Company, Erie, Pennsylvania – service speed 18 mph
Log – Lengthened 40 feet to 400 feet – gross tons 3,558 – capacity 32 railroad cars
 – Manitowoc Shipbuilding Corporation, Manitowoc, Wisconsin 1952/53
Cut down to a barge Milwaukee, Wisconsin fall 1974
Final status – Foundered 17 miles off Honduras, Caribbean Sea November 21, 1980

Wisconsin Maritime Museum

PERE MARQUETTE 21 ready for launch

Inland Seas Maritime Museum

PERE MARQUETTE 21

Inland Seas Maritime Museum

PERE MARQUETTE 21 in Manitowoc Shipbuilding dry dock 1956

PERE MARQUETTE 22 1924 Hull #210   Official No. 224122

    Customer – Pere Marquette Railway Company
    Plans and specifications – Steel carferry steamer – length 360 feet – beam 56 feet
        – depth 19.5 feet – gross tons 2,992 – net tons 1,501 – capacity four tracks,
        30 railroad cars – cost $800,000 – service speed 15 miles per hour
    Engines – Two triple expansion – 20.5 inch, 34 inch, 56 inch bores X 36 inch stroke
        – 2,700 horsepower
    Re-engined – Two Steeple compound – Unaflow – 19.5 inch, 43 inch bores X 46 inch stroke
        – Skinner Engine Company, Erie, Pennsylvania – service speed 18 mph 1952
    Log – Lengthened 40 feet to 400 feet – gross tons 3,558 – capacity 32 railroad cars
        – Manitowoc Shipbuilding Corporation, Manitowoc, Wisconsin 1952/53
    Cut down to a barge Milwaukee, Wisconsin fall 1973
    Last known status – Sold Panamanian December, 1974

ANN ARBOR #7 1925 Hull #214   Official No. 224430

    Customer – Ann Arbor Railway Company
    Plans and specifications – Steel carferry steamer – length 348 feet – beam 56 feet
        – depth 19.2 feet – gross tons 2,934 – net tons 1,426 – capacity four tracks,
        30 railroad cars
    Engines – Two triple expansion – 20.5 inch, 34 inch, 56 inch bores X 36 inch stroke
        – 2,700 horsepower
    Raised 3.5 feet – lengthened to 360 feet – re-engined four diesel electric motors
        – 1,500 horsepower – renamed VIKING 1965
    Current status – Idle – Menomine, Michigan

ANN ARBOR #7

CHARLES C. WEST 1925 Hull #216   Official No. 225066

Customer – Reiss Steamship Company or Rockport Steamship Company
Plans and specifications – Steel self-unloading steamer – length 456 feet – beam 60.1 feet – depth 29.1 feet – gross tons 6,644 – net tons 5,004
Engine – Triple expansion – 17.5 inch, 28.5 inch, 48 inch X 36 inch stroke – 2,000 horsepower
Lengthened – 592 feet – gross tons 8,481 – boom lengthened from 204 feet to 250 feet Manitowoc Shipbuilding, Manitowoc, Wisconsin 1948
Re-engined – Unaflow – 4 cylinder – 23.5 inch bore X 26 inch stroke – 4,200 horsepower 1952
Bow thruster added 1965
Final status – Scrapped Buffalo, New York 1979

CHARLES C. WEST

In 1925 the company built the eighth, ninth and tenth sections of the floating steel dry dock, reaching 600 feet in length.

Elias Gunnell died February 25, 1926.

MANITOWOC 1926 Hull #222 — Official No. 225671

Customer – Wabash Railway Company

Plans and specifications – Steel carferry steamer – length 358 feet – beam 56 feet – depth 19 feet – gross tons 3,093 – net tons – 1,391 – capacity four tracks, 32 railroad cars

Engines – Two fore and aft compound – 24 inch, 50 inch bores X 36 inch stroke – 2,600 horsepower

Last known status – Cut down to a car barge June, 1969

Great Lakes Marine Collection of the Milwaukee Public Library/Wisconsin Marine Historical Society
MANITOWOC

DANIEL MCCOOL 1926 Hull #223 — Official No. 226062

Customer – Medusa Cement Company

Plans and specifications – Steamer – length 152 feet – beam 33.5 feet – depth 15.0 feet – gross tons 649 – net tons 378

Re-engined and renamed J. B. JOHN 1951

Log – Laid idle in Manitowoc, Wisconsin 1955 to 1964

Converted to a self-unloader and renamed A. G. BRECKLING 1964

Converted to a cement self-unloader and renamed PEERLESS 1969

Final status – Sold in South America 1976

Wisconsin Maritime Museum

DANIEL MCCOOL

GRAND RAPIDS 1926 Hull #226   Official No. 226151

    Customer – Grand Trunk Railway System
    Plans and specifications – Steel carferry steamer – length 348 feet – beam 56 feet – depth 19 feet – gross tons 2,942 – net tons 1,488 – capacity four tracks, 30 railroad cars – service speed 17 miles per hour
    Engines – Two triple expansion – 20.5 inch, 34 inch, 56 inch bores X 36 inch stroke – 2,700 horsepower
Converted to oil 1947
Raised 4 feet early 1960s
Final status – Scrapped Port Colbourne, Ontario, Canada 1989

Historical Collection of the Great Lakes, Bowling Green State University

GRAND RAPIDS

MADISON 1927 Hull # 227   Official No. 226275

Customer – Grand Trunk Railway System

Plans and specifications – Steel carferry steamer – length 348 feet – beam 56 feet – depth 19 feet – gross tons 2,942 – net tons 1,488 – capacity four tracks, 30 railroad cars – service speed 17 miles per hour

Engines – Two triple expansion – 20.5 inch, 34 inch, 56 inch bores X 36 inch stroke – 2,700 horsepower

Final status – Scrapped Port Maitland, Nova Scotia, Canada 1994

Wisconsin Maritime Museum

Launch of the MADISON

PERE MARQUETTE 12 1927 Hull #234   Official No. 227030

Customer – Pere Marquette Railway Company

Plans and specifications – Steel carferry steamer – length 386 feet – beam 53 feet – depth 18 feet – gross tons 2,767 – net tons 1,123 – capacity three tracks, 27 railroad cars

Engines – Two triple expansion – 26.5 inch, 40 inch, 40 inch bores X 36 inch stroke – 3,600 horsepower

Wisconsin Maritime Museum

PERE MARQUETTE 12

CITY OF SAGINAW 31 1929 Hull #246   Official No. 229150

    Customer – Pere Marquette Railway Company
    Plans and specifications – Steel carferry steamer – length 382 feet – beam 58 feet – depth 20 feet – gross tons 3,327 – capacity four tracks, 32 railroad cars
    Engines – Two steam turbines – two AC generators – four Babcock and Wilcox water tube boilers – 3600 horsepower
    Special equipment – First commercial ship of the Great Lakes to have radar
    Log– Straight stack replaced with tapered stack in 1942
        Fire destroyed upper and forward works on July 29, 1971 at Manitowoc, Wisconsin
    Final status – Scrapped Costellon, Spain fall 1973

Wisconsin Maritime Museum

Launch of the CITY OF SAGINAW 31

CITY OF FLINT 32 1929 Hull #247   Official No. 229316

    Customer – Pere Marquette Railway Company
    Plans and specifications – Steel carferry steamer – length 382 feet – beam 58 feet – depth 20 feet – gross tons 3,327 – capacity four tracks, 32 railroad cars
    Engines – Two steam turbines – two AC generators – four Babcock and Wilcox water tube boilers – 3600 horsepower
    Special equipment – radar
    Straight stack replaced with tapered stack in 1942
    Cut down to a barge 1969
    Renamed ROANOKE 1970

Wisconsin Maritime Museum

CITY OF FLINT 32

CITY OF MILWAUKEE 1931 Hull # 261   Official No. 230448

    Customer – Grand Trunk Railway System
    Plans and specifications – Steel carferry steamer – length 348 feet – beam 56 feet
        – depth 19 feet – gross tons 2,942 – capacity four tracks, 30 railroad cars
        – service speed 17 miles per hour
    Engines – Two triple expansion – 20.5 inch, 34 inch, 56 inch bores X 36 inch stroke
        – 2,700 horsepower
    Current status – Museum – Manistee, Michigan 1994

Historical Collection of the Great Lakes, Bowling Green State University

CITY OF MILWAUKEE

Employment fell to a skeleton crew of 350 during the depression. The company's name was changed back to the Manitowoc Shipbuilding Company in 1937.

CITY OF MIDLAND 41 1941 Hull #311   Official No. 240326

    Customer – Pere Marquette Railway Company
    Plans and specifications – Steel carferry steamer – length 406 feet – beam 58 feet – depth 24.7 feet – gross tons 3,968 – capacity four tracks, 34 railroad cars and 50 automobiles – cost $1,970,000
    Engines – Two Skinner Unaflow – 5 cylinder – 25 inch bore X 30 inch stroke – 3,171 horsepower – Skinner Engine Company, Erie, Pennsylvania
    Log – Lost propeller in heavy ice February 19, 1977 – repaired Bay Shipbuilding April, 1977
    Renamed PERE MARQUETTE 41 – cut down to a barge in 1997 and 1998
    Current status – in service for the Pere Marquette Shipping Company
    Note: It was reported in the "Manitowoc Herald Times" that 15,000 people watched the launch of the CITY OF MIDLAND on, September 18, 1940. That was over half of the population of the county at that time.

Wisconsin Maritime Museum

Launch of the CITY OF MIDLAND 41

Wisconsin Maritime Museum

CITY OF MIDLAND 41 on sea trials

The 1870 dry dock was filled in in 1941 because its function had been taken over by the sectional steel floating dry docks. The land space was needed to fulfill a new Navy contract to build 10 and ultimately 28 submarines. Employment rose to over 6000 to construct these submarines. A Government Defense Housing Development program started June of 1941. Four hundred homes were built in an area on the southwest side of Manitowoc called Custerdale to house more employees. Employees were bussed in from Sheboygan, Green Bay, and Appleton. The submarines were not freight carrying vessels but are included because shipbuilding capabilities that were used to build the five large freighters in the following chapters were developed during the construction of these 28 submarines. These capabilities included welding, indoor prefabrication, large skilled labor force, and component transportation and placement equipment.

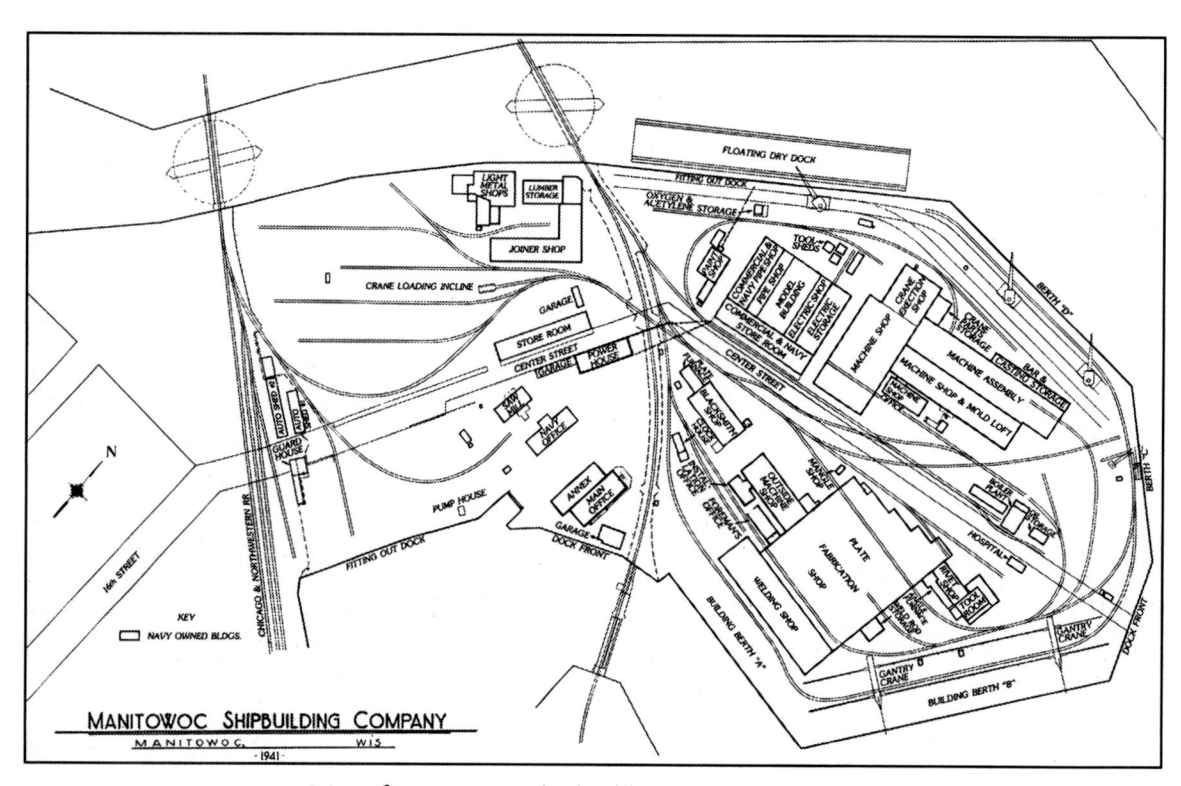

Map of Manitowoc Shipbuilding Company in 1941

PETO SS265 1942 Hull #313

    Customer – US Navy

    Plans and specifications – Steel submarine – length 312 feet – beam 27 feet – depth 15 feet – gross tons 1,526

    Engines – Two diesel electric – GM 16 278A V16 – 8.75 inch bore X 10.5 inch stroke – 1600 horsepower Allis-Chalmers direct current generators –2700 horsepower double armature direct current propulsion motors

    Final status – Stricken from Naval Record August 1, 1960 – scrapped November, 1960

Wisconsin Maritime Museum

Launch of the PETO

POGY SS266 1942 Hull #314

    Customer – US Navy

    Plans and specifications – Steel submarine – length 312 feet – beam 27 feet – depth 15 feet – gross tons 1,526

    Engines – Two diesel electric – GM 16 278A V16 – 8.75 inch bore X 10.5 inch stroke – 1600 horsepower Allis-Chalmers direct current generators – 2700 horsepower double armature direct current propulsion motors

    Final status – Stricken from Naval Record September 1, 1958

POMPON SS267 1942 Hull #315

    Customer – US Navy

    Plans and specifications – Steel submarine – length 312 feet – beam 27 feet – depth 15 feet – gross tons 1,526

    Engines – Two diesel electric – GM 16 278A V16 – 8.75 inch bore X 10.5 inch stroke – 1600 horsepower Allis-Chalmers direct current generators – 2700 horsepower double armature direct current propulsion motors

    Final status – Stricken from Naval Record April 1, 1960

Wisconsin Maritime Museum

The submarines were the first all-welded construction large vessels built in Manitowoc.

PUFFER SS268 1943 Hull #316

    Customer – US Navy

    Plans and specifications – Steel submarine – length 312 feet – beam 27 feet – depth 15 feet – gross tons 1,526

    Engines – Two diesel electric – GM 16 278A V16 – 8.75 inch bore X 10.5 inch stroke – 1600 horsepower Allis-Chalmers direct current generators – 2700 horsepower double armature direct current propulsion motors

    Final status – Stricken from Naval Record July 1, 1960 – scrapped 1961

RASHER SS269 1943 Hull #317

    Customer – US Navy

    Plans and specifications – Steel submarine – length 312 feet – beam 27 feet – depth 15 feet – gross tons 1,526

    Engines – Two diesel electric – GM 16 278A V16 – 8.75 inch bore X 10.5 inch stroke – 1600 horsepower Allis-Chalmers direct current generators – 2700 horsepower double armature direct current propulsion motors

    Final status – Stricken from Naval Record December 20, 1971

RATON SS270 1943 Hull #318

    Customer – US Navy

    Plans and specifications – Steel submarine – length 312 feet – beam 27 feet – depth 15 feet – gross tons 1,526

    Engines – Two diesel electric – GM 16 278A V16 – 8.75 inch bore X 10.5 inch stroke – 1600 horsepower Allis-Chalmers direct current generators – 2700 horsepower double armature direct current propulsion motors

    Final status – Stricken from Naval Record June 28, 1969

RAY SS271 1943 Hull #319

    Customer – US Navy

    Plans and specifications – Steel submarine – length 312 feet – beam 27 feet – depth 15 feet – gross tons 1,526

    Engines – Two diesel electric – GM 16 278A V16 – 8.75 inch bore X 10.5 inch stroke – 1600 horsepower Allis-Chalmers direct current generators – 2700 horsepower double armature direct current propulsion motors

    Final status – Stricken from Naval Record April 1, 1960

REDFIN SS272 1943 Hull #320

    Customer – US Navy

    Plans and specifications – Steel submarine – length 312 feet – beam 27 feet – depth 15 feet – gross tons 1,526

    Engines – Two diesel electric – GM 16 278A V16 – 8.75 inch bore X 10.5 inch stroke – 1600 horsepower Allis-Chalmers direct current generators – 2700 horsepower double armature direct current propulsion motors

    Final status – Stricken from Naval Record July 1, 1970 – dismantled

View of Manitowoc Shipbuilding yard with four submarines under construction in the summer of 1943.

RABALO SS273 1943 Hull #321

    Customer – US Navy

    Plans and specifications – Steel submarine – length 312 feet – beam 27 feet – depth 15 feet – gross tons 1,526

    Engines – Two diesel electric – GM 16 278A V16 – 8.75 inch bore X 10.5 inch stroke – 1600 horsepower Allis-Chalmers direct current generators – 2700 horsepower double armature direct current propulsion motors

    Final status – Sunk two miles off the west coast of Palawan Island, Pacific Ocean July 26, 1944

ROCK SS274 1943 Hull #322
> Customer – US Navy
> Plans and specifications – Steel submarine – length 312 feet – beam 27 feet – depth 15 feet – gross tons 1,526
> Engines – Two diesel electric – GM 16 278A V16 – 8.75 inch bore X 10.5 inch stroke – 1600 horsepower Allis-Chalmers direct current generators – 2700 horsepower double armature direct current propulsion motors
> Log – Rebuilt – lengthened 30 feet and converted to radar picket submarine – Philadelphia Navy Yard in 1951 and 1952
> Final status – Stricken from Naval Record October 26, 1969

GOLET SS361 1943 Hull #359
> Customer – US Navy
> Plans and specifications – Steel submarine – length 312 feet – beam 27 feet – depth 15 feet – gross tons 1,526
> Engines – Two diesel electric – GM 16 278A V16 – 8.75 inch bore X 10.5 inch stroke – 1600 horsepower Allis-Chalmers direct current generators – 2700 horsepower double armature direct current propulsion motors
> Final status – Sank north of Hanshu, Pacific Ocean June 14, 1944

Wisconsin Maritime Museum

Submarine sections are shown in various stages of prefabrication inside a building.

GUAVINA SS362 1943 Hull #360

Customer – US Navy

Plans and specifications – Steel submarine – length 312 feet – beam 27 feet – depth 15 feet – gross tons 1,526

Engines – Two diesel electric – GM 16 278A V16 – 8.75 inch bore X 10.5 inch stroke – 1600 horsepower Allis-Chalmers direct current generators – 2700 horsepower double armature direct current propulsion motors

Log – Refitted with snorkel March 1949

Final status – Stricken from Naval Record June 30, 1967

GUITARRO SS363 1943 Hull #361

Customer – US Navy

Plans and specifications – Steel submarine – length 312 feet – beam 27 feet – depth 15 feet – gross tons 1,526

Engines – Two diesel electric – GM 16 278A V16 – 8.75 inch bore X 10.5 inch stroke – 1600 horsepower Allis-Chalmers direct current generators – 2700 horsepower double armature direct current propulsion motors

Log – Converted to snorkel Mare Island, California 1952/53 – transferred to Turkey, August 7, 1955

Final status – Returned to US Navy and stricken from Naval Record January 1, 1972

HAMMERHEAD SS364 1943 Hull #362

Customer – US Navy

Plans and specifications – Steel submarine – length 312 feet – beam 27 feet – depth 15 feet – gross tons 1,526

Engines – Two diesel electric – GM 16 278A V16 – 8.75 inch bore X 10.5 inch stroke – 1600 horsepower Allis-Chalmers direct current generators – 2700 horsepower double armature direct current propulsion motors

Log – Transferred to Turkey October 23, 1954

Final status – Returned to US Navy and stricken from Naval Record January 1, 1972.

HARDHEAD SS365 1944 Hull #363

Customer – US Navy

Plans and specifications – Steel submarine – length 312 feet – beam 27 feet – depth 15 feet – gross tons 1,526

Engines – Two diesel electric – GM 16 278A V16 – 8.75 inch bore X 10.5 inch stroke – 1600 horsepower Allis-Chalmers direct current generators – 2700 horsepower double armature direct current propulsion motors

Log – Transferred to Turkey October 23, 1954

Final status – Stricken from Naval Record July 26, 1972

HAWKBILL SS366 1944 Hull #364

Customer – US Navy

Plans and specifications – Steel submarine – length 312 feet – beam 27 feet – depth 15 feet – gross tons 1,526

Engines – Two diesel electric – GM 16 278A V16 – 8.75 inch bore X 10.5 inch stroke – 1600 horsepower Allis-Chalmers direct current generators – 2700 horsepower double armature direct current propulsion motors

Log – Transferred to Netherlands April 21, 1953

Final status – Returned to US Navy and stricken from Naval Record February 2, 1970

Wisconsin Maritime Museum

A typical crew of skilled workers are shown working on a submarine.

ICEFISH SS367 1944 Hull #365

    Customer – US Navy

    Plans and specifications – Steel submarine – length 312 feet – beam 27 feet – depth 15 feet – gross tons 1,526

    Engines – Two diesel electric – GM 16 278A V16 – 8.75 inch bore X 10.5 inch stroke – 1600 horsepower Allis-Chalmers direct current generators – 2700 horsepower double armature direct current propulsion motors

    Log – Transferred to Netherlands February 21, 1953

    Final status – Returned to US Navy and stricken from Naval Record July 5, 1971

JALLAO SS368 1944 Hull #366

    Customer – US Navy

    Plans and specifications – Steel submarine – length 312 feet – beam 27 feet – depth 15 feet – gross tons 1,526

    Engines – Two diesel electric – GM 16 278A V16 – 8.75 inch bore X 10.5 inch stroke – 1600 horsepower Allis-Chalmers direct current generators – 2700 horsepower double armature direct current propulsion motors

    Final status – Transferred to Spain June 1974

KETE SS369 1944 Hull #367

    Customer – US Navy

    Plans and specifications – Steel submarine – length 312 feet – beam 27 feet – depth 15 feet – gross tons 1,526

    Engines – Two diesel electric – GM 16 278A V16 – 8.75 inch bore X 10.5 inch stroke – 1600 horsepower Allis-Chalmers direct current generators – 2700 horsepower double armature direct current propulsion motors

    Final status – Sank Nnsec Shoto Islands, Pacific Ocean March 20, 1945

KRAKEN SS370 1944 Hull #368
    Customer – US Navy
    Plans and specifications – Steel submarine – length 312 feet – beam 27 feet – depth 15 feet – gross tons 1,526
    Engines – Two diesel electric – GM 16 278A V16 – 8.75 inch bore X 10.5 inch stroke – 1600 horsepower Allis-Chalmers direct current generators – 2700 horsepower double armature direct current propulsion motors
    Final status – Transferred to Spain October 24, 1959

LAGARTO SS371 1944 Hull #369
    Customer – US Navy
    Plans and specifications – Steel submarine – length 312 feet – beam 27 feet – depth 15 feet – gross tons 1,526
    Engines – Two diesel electric – GM 16 278A V16 – 8.75 inch bore X 10.5 inch stroke – 1600 horsepower Allis-Chalmers direct current generators – 2700 horsepower double armature direct current propulsion motors
    Final status – Sank Gulf of Siam, Indian Ocean May 4, 1945

LAMPREY SS372 1944 Hull #370
    Customer – US Navy
    Plans and specifications – Steel submarine – length 312 feet – beam 27 feet – depth 15 feet – gross tons 1,526
    Engines – Two diesel electric – GM 16 278A V16 – 8.75 inch bore X 10.5 inch stroke – 1600 horsepower Allis-Chalmers direct current generators – 2700 horsepower double armature direct current propulsion motors
    Log – Loaned to Argentina July 25, 1960
    Final status – Returned to US Navy and stricken from Naval Record September 1, 1971 – scrapped in Argentina 1971

LIZARDFISH SS373 1944 Hull #371
    Customer – US Navy
    Plans and specifications – Steel submarine – length 312 feet – beam 27 feet – depth 15 feet – gross tons 1,526
    Engines – Two diesel electric – GM 16 278A V16 – 8.75 inch bore X 10.5 inch stroke – 1600 horsepower Allis-Chalmers direct current generators – 2700 horsepower double armature direct current propulsion motors
    Log – Loaned to Italy January 9, 1960
    Final status – Transferred to Italy July 13, 1979

LOGGERHEAD SS374 1944 Hull #372
    Customer – US Navy
    Plans and specifications – Steel submarine – length 312 feet – beam 27 feet – depth 15 feet – gross tons 1,526
    Engines – Two diesel electric – GM 16 278A V16 – 8.75 inch bore X 10.5 inch stroke – 1600 horsepower Allis-Chalmers direct current generators – 2700 horsepower double armature direct current propulsion motors
    Final status – Stricken from Naval Record June 30, 1967 – scrapped early 1969

MACABI SS375 1944 Hull #373

    Customer – US Navy

    Plans and specifications – Steel submarine – length 312 feet – beam 27 feet – depth 15 feet – gross tons 1,526

    Engines – Two diesel electric – GM 16 278A V16 – 8.75 inch bore X 10.5 inch stroke – 1600 horsepower Allis-Chalmers direct current generators – 2700 horsepower double armature direct current propulsion motors

    Log – Transferred to Argentina June 23, 1960

    Final status – Scuttled off South Georgia Island, Atlantic Ocean 1985

Transporting a completed submarine section to the final assembly dock

Placing a submarine section on the final assembly dock

MAPIRO SS376 1944/45 Hull #374

    Customer – US Navy

    Plans and specifications – Steel submarine – length 312 feet – beam 27 feet – depth 15 feet – gross tons 1,526

    Engines – Two diesel electric – GM 16 278A V16 – 8.75 inch bore X 10.5 inch stroke – 1600 horsepower Allis-Chalmers direct current generators – 2700 horsepower double armature direct current propulsion motors

    Final status – Transferred to Turkey March 18, 1960

MENHADEN SS377 1944/45 Hull #376

    Customer – US Navy

    Plans and specifications – Steel submarine – length 312 feet – beam 27 feet – depth 15 feet – gross tons 1,526

    Engines – Two diesel electric – GM 16 278A V16 – 8.75 inch bore X 10.5 inch stroke – 1600 horsepower Allis-Chalmers direct current generators – 2700 horsepower double armature direct current propulsion motors

    Log – Converted to snorkel 1952

    Current status – Training and test vessel Seattle, Washington 1985

MERO SS378 1945 Hull #376

    Customer – US Navy

    Plans and specifications – Steel submarine – length 312 feet – beam 27 feet – depth 15 feet – gross tons 1,526

    Engines – Two diesel electric – GM 16 278A V16 – 8.75 inch bore X 10.5 inch stroke – 1600 horsepower Allis-Chalmers direct current generators – 2700 horsepower double armature direct current propulsion motors

    Log – Converted to snorkel 1952

    Final status – Transferred to Turkey April 20, 1960

Wisconsin Maritime Museum

MERO, the last submarine built in Manitowoc, on sea trials

NEEDLEFISH SS379 1945 Hull #377

Not built, contract cancelled

Customer – US Navy

Plans and specifications – Steel submarine – length 312 feet – beam 27 feet – depth 15 feet – gross tons 1,526

Engines – Two diesel electric – GM 16 278A V16 – 8.75 inch bore X 10.5 inch stroke – 1600 horsepower Allis-Chalmers direct current generators – 2700 horsepower double armature direct current propulsion motors

NERKA SS380 1945 Hull #378

Not built, contract cancelled

Customer – US Navy

Plans and specifications – Steel submarine – length 312 feet – beam 27 feet – depth 15 feet – gross tons 1,526

Engines – Two diesel electric – GM 16 278A V16 – 8.75 inch bore X 10.5 inch stroke – 1600 horsepower Allis-Chalmers direct current generators – 2700 horsepower double armature direct current propulsion motors

PERE MARQUETTE 10 1945 Hull #393   Official No. 249091

Customer – Pere Marquette Railway Company

Plans and specifications – Steel carferry steamer – length 386 feet – beam 53 feet – depth 18 feet – gross tons 2,769 – capacity three tracks, 27 railroad cars

Engines – Two Unaflow – 3 cylinder – 25 inch bore X 24 inch stroke – Skinner Engine Company Erie, Pennsylvania

Last known status – Cut down to a car barge 1974

Historical Collection of the Great Lakes, Bowling Green State University

PERE MARQUETTE 10

ADAM E. CORNELIUS II 1948   Official No. 205239

    Customer – Boland and Cornelius
    Converted to self-unloader – lengthened 48 feet
    Final status – Scrapped Taiwan October, 1988

Wisconsin Maritime Museum

ADAM E. CORNELIUS II after conversion to a self-unloader

PETER REISS 1949

    Customer – Reiss Steamship Company
    Converted to a self-unloader
    Final status – Scrapped Port Colbourne, Ontario 1973

The Manitowoc Company, Inc. was formed with Manitowoc Shipbuilding, Inc. as a subsidiary in 1952.

WILLIAM A. REISS 1953/54   Official No. 225045

    Customer – Reiss Steamship company
    Re-engined – DeLaval geared steam turbine – 5,000 horsepower
    Raised 7.5 feet – new depth 39.5 feet – cost $623,000
    Log – Laid up Toledo, Ohio 1981
    Final status – Scrapped Far East 1994

ANN ARBOR #6 1958   Official No. 214656

    Customer – Ann Arbor Railroad
    Lengthened 34 feet, raised 2 feet – gross tons + 1,200
    Re-engined – Nordberg diesel – 2,500 horsepower – controllable pitch propellers
    Renamed ARTHUR K. ATKINSON
    Current status – St. Marys River, De Tour Village, Michigan 2006

WABASH 1962   Official No. 226597

    Customer – Ann Arbor Railroad
    Raised 3.5 feet
    Renamed CITY OF GREEN BAY
    Final status – Scrapped 1974 Spain

CHAPTER 2

JOHN G. MUNSON

JOHN G. MUNSON 1952 Hull # 415   Official No. 264136

Mr. John Gephart Munson was born January 6, 1885 in Bellefonte, Pennsylvania and received his Bachelor of Science Degree in Civil Engineering from Yale in 1905. He joined the Michigan Limestone and Chemical Company in 1919 as operating manager and in 1925 became its vice president. In 1928 he was elected president of both Michigan Limestone and Chemical Company and Bradley Transportation Division. He served in that capacity until 1939 when he became vice president in charge of raw materials for the parent United States Steel Corporation. He continued in that post until retiring in 1951. Before the vessel was completed, Mr. Munson died on March 28, 1952.

Manitowoc Shipbuilding, Inc., Manitowoc, Wisconsin
- Customer – Bradley Transportation Line, Subsidiary of United States Steel
- Plans and specifications – Steel self-unloader – length 666 feet – length between perpendiculars 650 feet – length of keel 640 feet – beam 72 feet – depth – 36 feet – draft 25 feet – gross tons 13,143 – net tons 8,116 – displacement at 25 feet draft 30,800 tons – cargo capacity 25,500 tons – forward boom length 250 feet – hatches, 18 on 24 foot centers, 45 feet 9 inches wide X 12 feet long – service speed 16.25 miles per hour – total crew 36 – cost $6,500,000 – 30 miles of marine wire – 6 miles of piping – 180,000 rivets – 100 miles of weld
- Engine – General Electric – compound steam turbine – double reduction gear – 7,700 horsepower maximum – 7,000 horsepower normal
- Boilers – Two Foster-Wheeler – water tube
- Fuel – coal
- Special equipment – Radar – master gyro compass – automatic tank sounding – course recorder – radio direction finder – radio telephone
- Construction
    - Keel laid – March 7, 1951
    - Launch – November 28, 1951
    - Sea trials – August 12, 1952
    - Commissioned – August 20, 1952
    - Delivered – August 21, 1952
- Log – Maiden voyage – Manitowoc, Wisconsin to Calcite Harbor, Michigan August 21, 1952. The JOHN G. MUNSON loaded 21,011 tons of Limestone at Calcite, Michigan on July 4, 1953, which was a record cargo that stood until 1966.
    Bow thruster was added in 1966.
    Lengthened to 786 feet – length between perpendiculars 752 feet – gross tons – 15,179 – net tons 11,330 – hatches, 22 on 24 foot centers, 45 feet 9 inches wide X 12 feet long Fraser Shipyard, Superior, Wisconsin 1975/76.
    Converted to fuel oil – 1976

USS Great Lakes Fleet – 1980
Stern thruster added – 1986
Current status – in service for USS Great Lakes Fleet Inc.

Wisconsin Maritime Museum & The Manitowoc Company, Inc.

The keel blocks are all in place for the JOHN G. MUNSON February 28, 1951.

Wisconsin Maritime Museum & The Manitowoc Company, Inc.

The keel is being laid for the JOHN G. MUNSON March 7, 1951.

The first two pieces of the JOHN G. MUNSON are being welded together March 7, 1951.

Chapter 2: JOHN G. MUNSON 131

Wisconsin Maritime Museum & The Manitowoc Company, Inc.
More bottom plates are being welded on the JOHN G. MUNSON March 23, 1951.

Wisconsin Maritime Museum & The Manitowoc Company, Inc.
The first double bottom and side sections are being assembled of the JOHN G. MUNSON April 6, 1951.

Wisconsin Maritime Museum & The Manitowoc Company, Inc.

Port and starboard double bottom and side sections now appear
on the JOHN G. MUNSON April 16, 1951.

Wisconsin Maritime Museum & The Manitowoc Company, Inc.

Looking from the bow, more double bottom and side sections are
in place on the JOHN G. MUNSON May 11, 1951.

Chapter 2: JOHN G. MUNSON 133

Wisconsin Maritime Museum & The Manitowoc Company, Inc.

Top side sections on starboard side of the JOHN G. MUNSON looking at the stern May 11, 1951.

Wisconsin Maritime Museum & The Manitowoc Company, Inc.

More side sections and top sections are shown on the JOHN G. MUNSON looking at the stern June 8, 1951.

Wisconsin Maritime Museum & The Manitowoc Company, Inc.

More top sides with deck beams and first stern frame in the foreground of the JOHN G. MUNSON June 15, 1951.

Wisconsin Maritime Museum & The Manitowoc Company, Inc.

A side view of the JOHN G. MUNSON looking at the stern June 22, 1951.

Chapter 2: JOHN G. MUNSON 135

Wisconsin Maritime Museum & The Manitowoc Company, Inc.

Stern view showing the stern beginning to take shape and a cargo hold
bulkhead of the JOHN G. MUNSON July 6, 1951.

Wisconsin Maritime Museum & The Manitowoc Company, Inc.

Aerial view of the JOHN G. MUNSON showing the double V cargo
hold bottom and some deck hatch openings July 10, 1951.

136　Freighters of Manitowoc

Wisconsin Maritime Museum & The Manitowoc Company, Inc.
Plating is being fit on the stern piece of the JOHN G. MUNSON August 1, 1951.

Wisconsin Maritime Museum & The Manitowoc Company, Inc.
Stern view showing more stern shape and ballast tanks of the JOHN G. MUNSON August 10, 1951.

Wisconsin Maritime Museum & The Manitowoc Company, Inc.

The prefabricated stern piece is being hoisted into place on the JOHN G. MUNSON August 19, 1951.

Wisconsin Maritime Museum & The Manitowoc Company, Inc.

Bow view showing the bow taking shape and completed mid body
of the JOHN G. MUNSON August 31, 1951.

Wisconsin Maritime Museum & The Manitowoc Company, Inc.

The bow of the JOHN G. MUNSON is more complete on September 14, 1951.

Wisconsin Maritime Museum & The Manitowoc Company, Inc.

The hull is being built to the stern piece of the JOHN G. MUNSON September 21, 1951.

Chapter 2: JOHN G. MUNSON 139

Wisconsin Maritime Museum & The Manitowoc Company, Inc.
The upper stern piece is being fabricated on the JOHN G. MUNSON September 21, 1951.

Wisconsin Maritime Museum & The Manitowoc Company, Inc.
A section of the bow of the JOHN G. MUNSON is being fabricated September 29, 1951.

Wisconsin Maritime Museum & The Manitowoc Company, Inc.
The bow taking shape and more completed mid body of the JOHN G. MUNSON October 5, 1951.

Chapter 2: JOHN G. MUNSON 141

Wisconsin Maritime Museum & The Manitowoc Company, Inc.
The main bow section of the JOHN G. MUNSON is being rotated October 10, 1951.

Wisconsin Maritime Museum & The Manitowoc Company, Inc.
The bow of the JOHN G. MUNSON is being hoisted into position October 11, 1951

Chapter 2: JOHN G. MUNSON

Wisconsin Maritime Museum & The Manitowoc Company, Inc.

The stern and mid body of the JOHN G. MUNSON are nearly completed October 19, 1951.

Wisconsin Maritime Museum & The Manitowoc Company, Inc.

Plating is being applied to the upper stern of the JOHN G. MUNSON October 26, 1951.

Wisconsin Maritime Museum & The Manitowoc Company, Inc.

Main bow section added and more plating on the bow of the JOHN G. MUNSON October 26, 1951.

Wisconsin Maritime Museum & The Manitowoc Company, Inc.

Plating is being applied to the upper bow of the JOHN G. MUNSON November 9, 1951.

Wisconsin Maritime Museum & The Manitowoc Company, Inc.
Early launch day of the JOHN G. MUNSON November 28, 1951.

Wisconsin Maritime Museum & The Manitowoc Company, Inc.
Workers are pounding wedges to raise the JOHN G. MUNSON
onto the launch ways November 28, 1951.

Wisconsin Maritime Museum & The Manitowoc Company, Inc.

Here is some of the anxious crowd waiting the launch of the JOHN G. MUNSON November 28, 1951.

Wisconsin Maritime Museum & The Manitowoc Company, Inc.

Mrs. John G. Munson, with John E. Thiell, is christening the
JOHN G. MUNSON November 28, 1951.

Chapter 2: JOHN G. MUNSON

Wisconsin Maritime Museum & The Manitowoc Company, Inc.

The JOHN G. MUNSON launch November 28, 1951.

Wisconsin Maritime Museum & The Manitowoc Company, Inc.

The JOHN G. MUNSON is being pushed back to the dock after launch November 28, 1951.

Wisconsin Maritime Museum & The Manitowoc Company, Inc.
Arial view of the JOHN G. MUNSON beginning upper works construction December 10, 1951.

Wisconsin Maritime Museum & The Manitowoc Company, Inc.
Aft superstructure is taking shape on the JOHN G. MUNSON December 28, 1951.

Chapter 2: JOHN G. MUNSON 149

Wisconsin Maritime Museum & The Manitowoc Company, Inc.

The main drive gear being installed on the front of the propeller
shaft of the JOHN G. MUNSON December 29, 1951.

Wisconsin Maritime Museum & The Manitowoc Company, Inc.

Arial view of the JOHN G. MUNSON with deck hatches in place and
more fore and aft upper works completed February 14, 1952.

Installing part of the reduction gear between the steam turbines and the propeller shaft on the JOHN G. MUNSON March 25, 1952.

The stern decks are being finished on the JOHN G. MUNSON March 25, 1952.

Chapter 2: JOHN G. MUNSON

Wisconsin Maritime Museum & The Manitowoc Company, Inc.

More fore and aft superstructure is completed and the self-unloading boom is under construction of the JOHN G. MUNSON April 30, 1952.

Wisconsin Maritime Museum & The Manitowoc Company, Inc.

The name is being painted on the stern of the JOHN G. MUNSON May 13, 1952.

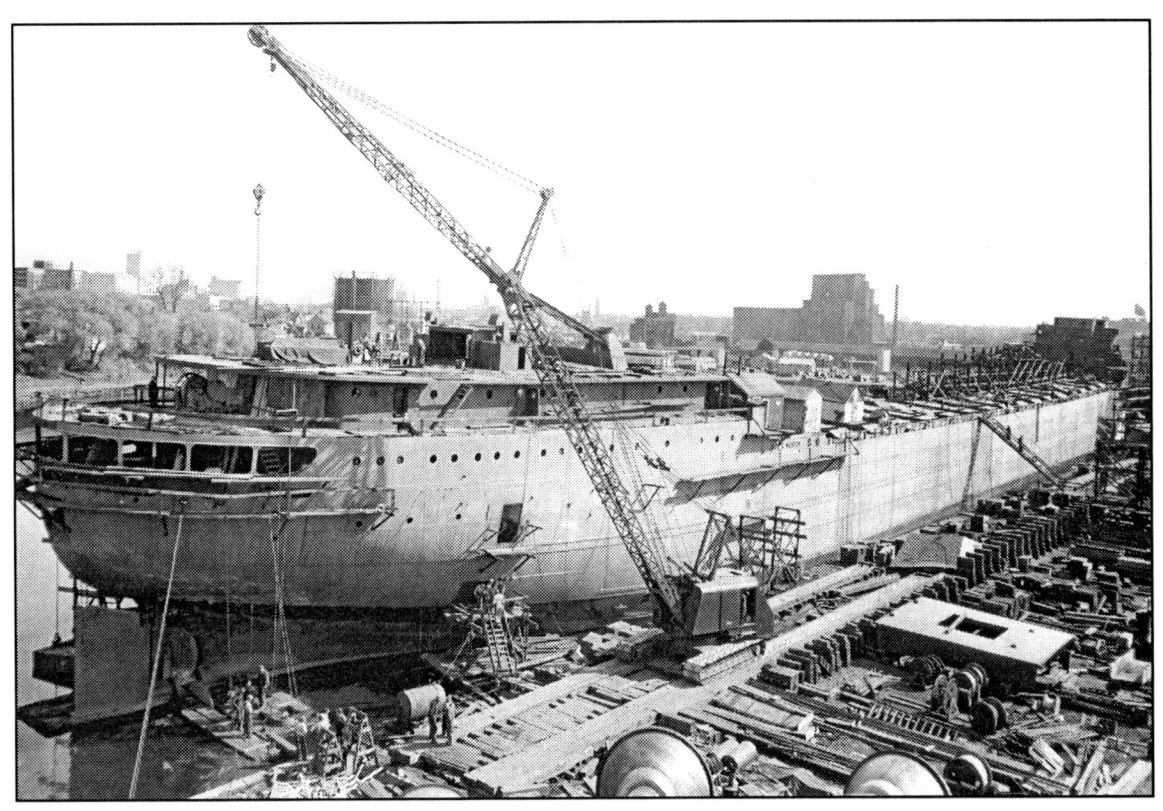

Wisconsin Maritime Museum & The Manitowoc Company, Inc.

Bow view of the JOHN G. MUNSON showing the forward
quarters and pilot house being finished May 13, 1952.

Wisconsin Maritime Museum & The Manitowoc Company, Inc.

The stack is in place of the JOHN G. MUNSON May 21, 1952.

Chapter 2: JOHN G. MUNSON 153

Wisconsin Maritime Museum & The Manitowoc Company, Inc.
The upper self-unloading machinery is being installed on the JOHN G. MUNSON June 9, 1952.

Wisconsin Maritime Museum & The Manitowoc Company, Inc.
The self-unloading elevator and boom are nearly finished on the JOHN G. MUNSON August 8, 1952.

Wisconsin Maritime Museum & The Manitowoc Company, Inc.

The completed JOHN G. MUNSON being towed through the 8th Street bridge, downtown Manitowoc August 12, 1952.

Wisconsin Maritime Museum & The Manitowoc Company, Inc.

The JOHN G. MUNSON is departing the Manitowoc Harbor on sea trials August 12, 1952.

Chapter 2: JOHN G. MUNSON 155

Wisconsin Maritime Museum & The Manitowoc Company, Inc.

One of the two tunnels of the JOHN G. MUNSON that provides an internal protected passageway from the bow to the stern August 21, 1952.

Wisconsin Maritime Museum & The Manitowoc Company, Inc.

View of the coal stokers on the JOHN G. MUNSON August 21, 1952.

Wisconsin Maritime Museum & The Manitowoc Company, Inc.
The self-unloading system conveyers are shown on the JOHN G. MUNSON August 21, 1952.

Wisconsin Maritime Museum & The Manitowoc Company, Inc.
This is the cargo conveyer drive of the JOHN G. MUNSON August 21, 1952.

Wisconsin Maritime Museum & The Manitowoc Company, Inc.

Shown is the electromechanical steering gear on the JOHN G. MUNSON August 21, 1952.

Wisconsin Maritime Museum & The Manitowoc Company, Inc.

View of the steam turbine engine room with the low pressure turbine in
the foreground on the JOHN G. MUNSON August 21, 1952.

Wisconsin Maritime Museum & The Manitowoc Company, Inc.

View of the steam turbine engine room with the high pressure turbine in the foreground on the JOHN G. MUNSON August 21, 1952.

Wisconsin Maritime Museum & The Manitowoc Company, Inc.

The engine control panel in the engine room on the JOHN G. MUNSON August 21, 1952.

Chapter 2: JOHN G. MUNSON

Wisconsin Maritime Museum & The Manitowoc Company, Inc.

The boiler control panel, with stokers in the background, is shown on the JOHN G. MUNSON August 21, 1952.

Wisconsin Maritime Museum & The Manitowoc Company, Inc.

View of the galley on the JOHN G. MUNSON August 21, 1952.

Wisconsin Maritime Museum & The Manitowoc Company, Inc.
Officers' dining room on the JOHN G. MUNSON August 21, 1952.

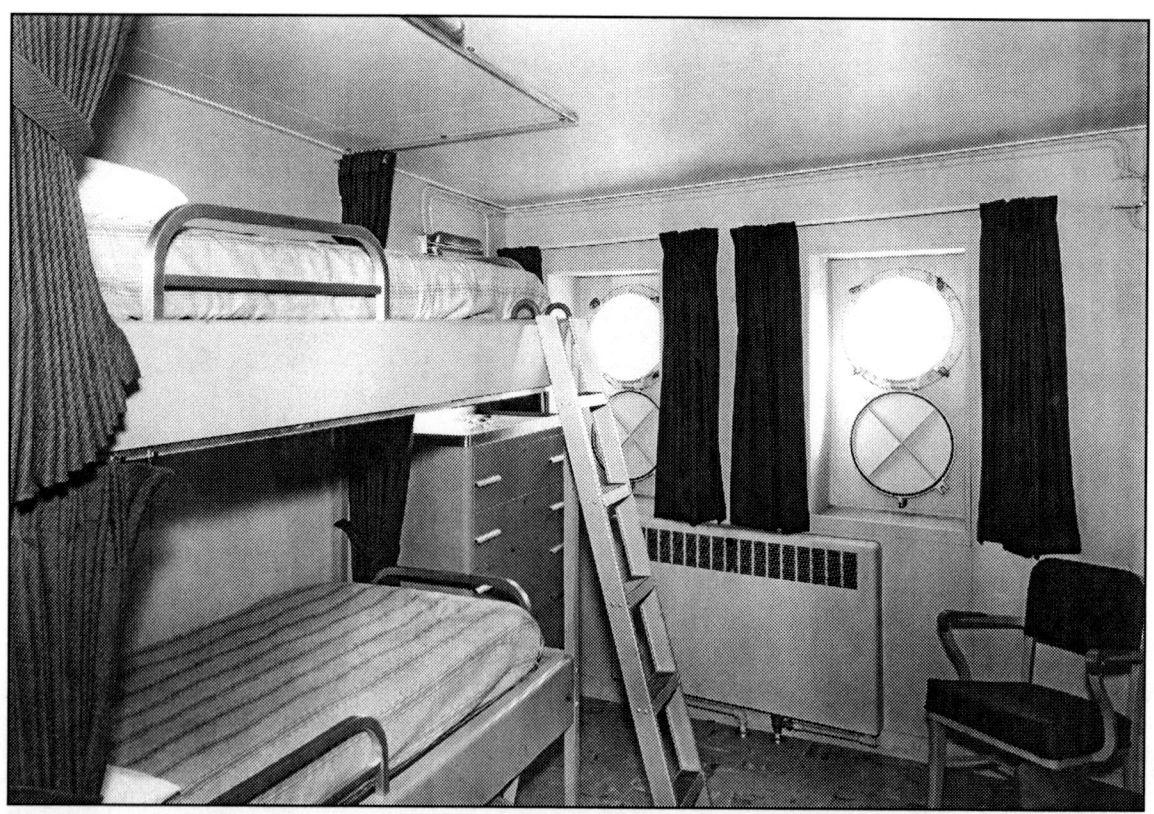

Wisconsin Maritime Museum & The Manitowoc Company, Inc.
Typical crew's quarters on the JOHN G. MUNSON August 21, 1952.

Wisconsin Maritime Museum & The Manitowoc Company, Inc.

View of the guest lounge on the JOHN G. MUNSON August 21, 1952.

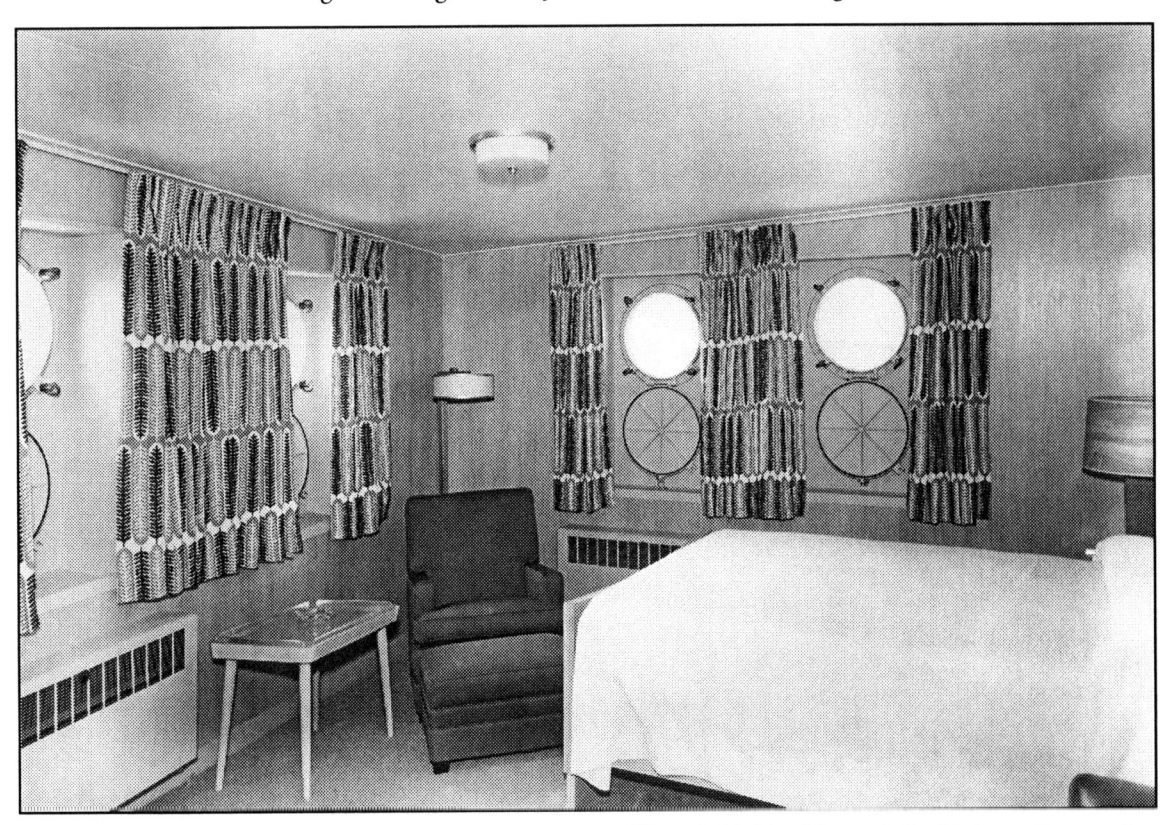

Wisconsin Maritime Museum & The Manitowoc Company, Inc.

The captain's quarters are shown on the JOHN G. MUNSON August 21, 1952.

Wisconsin Maritime Museum & The Manitowoc Company, Inc.

Navigation room is shown, with the gyro compass to the right, aft of the pilot house on the JOHN G. MUNSON August 21, 1952.

Wisconsin Maritime Museum & The Manitowoc Company, Inc.

View of the helm of the JOHN G. MUNSON looking to the port aft August 21, 1952.

Wisconsin Maritime Museum & The Manitowoc Company, Inc.

View of the helm of the JOHN G. MUNSON looking port forward August 21, 1952.

Wisconsin Maritime Museum & The Manitowoc Company, Inc.

Looking aft over the self-unloading boom of the JOHN G. MUNSON while docked on the south side of the Manitowoc River adjacent to where some of the old shipyards in Chapter 1 were located August 21, 1952.

Chapter 2: JOHN G. MUNSON 165

Wisconsin Maritime Museum & The Manitowoc Company, Inc.

The JOHN G. MUNSON at the dock in the Manitowoc River is
building up steam for departure August 21, 1952.

Wisconsin Maritime Museum & The Manitowoc Company, Inc.

The JOHN G. MUNSON is leaving Manitowoc on her maiden voyage August 21, 1952.

Wisconsin Maritime Museum & The Manitowoc Company, Inc.
Parting shot August 21, 1952.

Chapter 3

JOHN J. BOLAND III

JOHN J. BOLAND III 1953 Hull # 417   Official No. 266270

    Mr. John James Boland was born in Buffalo, New York on September 20, 1875. He began his career in Great Lakes shipping in 1895 when he organized a vessel brokerage business in Buffalo, New York. In 1902 he purchased the steamer YALE, one of the first steel ships on the Great Lakes. In 1904 he formed a partnership with Adam E. Cornelius becoming president of the firm of Boland and Cornelius. In 1907, Boland and Cornelius became the American Steamship Company, now the largest self-unloader fleet on the Great Lakes. As chairman of the board of the American Steamship Company, Mr. Boland was a major influence in the expansion of the self-unloading vessels on the Great Lakes and was also a director of the American Shipbuilding Company, a major competitor to Manitowoc Shipbuilding Company. John J. Boland died on October 3, 1956.

    Manitowoc Shipbuilding, Inc., Manitowoc, Wisconsin
        Customer – American Steamship Company
        Designer – Manitowoc Shipbuilding Company
        Plans and specifications – Steel self-unloader – length 639 feet – length between perpendiculars 613 feet – beam 72 feet – depth – 36 feet – draft 25 feet – gross tons 12,557 – net tons 9,038 – cargo capacity 18,000 tons limestone or 16,500 tons coal – forward boom length 258.5 feet – unloading rates – 3700 tons per hour coal and 4000 tons per hour limestone – hatches, 30 on 12 foot centers, 45 feet 9 inches wide X 12 feet long – service speed 16.25 miles per hour – total crew 41 – cost $6,500,000 – 6100 tons of steel was used in construction
        Engine – DeLaval steam compound turbine – double reduction gear – 7,700 horespower maximum – 7,000 horsepower normal
        Boilers – Two Foster-Wheeler – water tube
        Propeller – 4 blade
        Fuel – coal – capacity 25, 200 cubic feet
        Special equipment – Radar – master gyro compass – automatic tank sounding – radio direction finder – radio telephone
        Construction
            Keel laid – March 15, 1952
            Launch – May 9, 1953
            Sea trials – September 22, 1953
            Commissioned – September 23, 1953
            Delivered – September 23, 1953
        Log – The JOHN J. BOLAND loaded its initial cargo on September 25, 1953 at Port Inland, Michigan
            Bottom repaired at Fraser Yard Superior, Wisconsin 1962
            Bow thruster 850 horsepower 1965
            Converted to fuel oil with 105,000 gallon capacity 1971
            New self-unloading boom Sturgeon Bay, Wisconsin March 1974
            Bottom repaired at South Chicago yard 1975

Hull repaired at Fraser Yard Superior, Wisconsin 1985
Laid up 1987 to 1992
Back in service carrying limestone 1992
Sold to Black Creek Shipping Company – renamed SAGINAW 2001
Current status – in service for Lower Lakes Towing LTD.

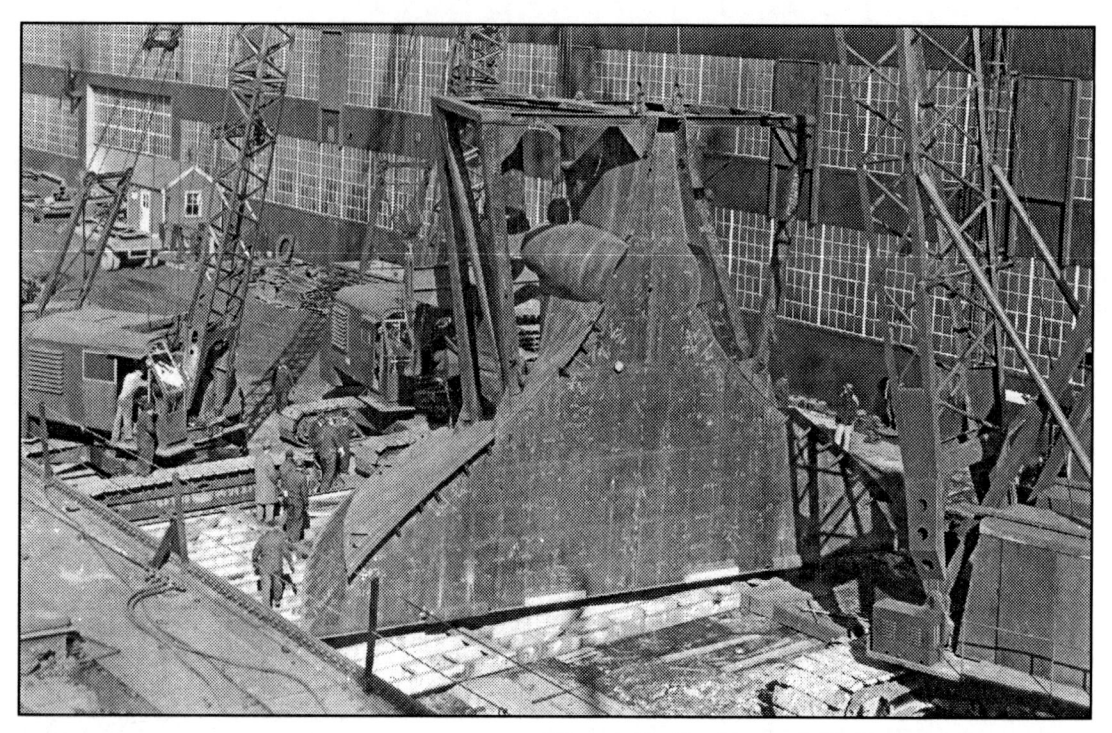

Wisconsin Maritime Museum & The Manitowoc Company, Inc.

The prefabricated stern piece of the JOHN J. BOLAND is being readied to move into position March 15, 1952.

Wisconsin Maritime Museum & The Manitowoc Company, Inc.

The prefabricated stern piece of the JOHN J. BOLAND is being positioned March 15, 1952. Notice that there is no construction in front of it. Instead of the keel, this was the first piece of the JOHN J. BOLAND put in place.

Wisconsin Maritime Museum & The Manitowoc Company, Inc.

Armin Pitz and two other Manitowoc Shipbuilding managers are discussing the placement of the stern piece of the JOHN J. BOLAND March 15, 1952.

Wisconsin Maritime Museum & The Manitowoc Company, Inc.

The stern piece of the JOHN J. BOLAND is in place March 15, 1952, with the unfinished JOHN G. MUNSON in the water in the background.

Wisconsin Maritime Museum & The Manitowoc Company, Inc.

Hull frames are being placed in front of the stern piece of the JOHN J. BOLAND April 22, 1952.

Wisconsin Maritime Museum & The Manitowoc Company, Inc.

The stern of the JOHN J. BOLAND taking shape with another prefabricated section on a transport tractor in the foreground May 13, 1952.

Wisconsin Maritime Museum & The Manitowoc Company, Inc.

Keel construction in front of the more completed stern of the JOHN J. BOLAND May 13, 1952.

Wisconsin Maritime Museum & The Manitowoc Company, Inc.

Taken from the deck of the adjacent JOHN G. MUNSON, more keel and double bottom is in place with the stern most tanks now in place May 21, 1952.

Wisconsin Maritime Museum & The Manitowoc Company, Inc.

Crews are working on both the JOHN G. MUNSON and the JOHN J. BOLAND June 9, 1952. Note the crane on the JOHN J. BOLAND poised to lift onto the JOHN G. MUNSON as well as all of the welding cable over the side of the MUNSON.

Chapter 3: JOHN J. BOLAND III

Wisconsin Maritime Museum & The Manitowoc Company, Inc.

More double bottom and side sections of the JOHN J. BOLAND looking at the stern June 25, 1952.

Wisconsin Maritime Museum & The Manitowoc Company, Inc.

More double bottom and side sections with the first deck beams over
the stern of the JOHN J. BOLAND July 2, 1952.

Wisconsin Maritime Museum & The Manitowoc Company, Inc.

Midship construction of bottom plates, double bottom and sides with fully decked stern of the JOHN J. BOLAND August 20, 1952. Notice that the JOHN G. MUNSON is no longer in the background.

Wisconsin Maritime Museum & The Manitowoc Company, Inc.

The framed bow piece of the JOHN J. BOLAND is shown August 20, 1952.

Chapter 3: JOHN J. BOLAND III 175

Wisconsin Maritime Museum & The Manitowoc Company, Inc.
The bow piece of the JOHN J. BOLAND is nearly plated September 6, 1952.

Wisconsin Maritime Museum & The Manitowoc Company, Inc.
More double bottom and side sections of the JOHN J. BOLAND September 6, 1952 with the next prefabricated piece in the foreground.

Wisconsin Maritime Museum & The Manitowoc Company, Inc.
View of the stern of the JOHN J. BOLAND September 6, 1952.

Wisconsin Maritime Museum & The Manitowoc Company, Inc.
The engine and boiler room with the low pressure steam turbine gearbox being hoisted into place on the JOHN J. BOLAND September 6, 1952.

Wisconsin Maritime Museum & The Manitowoc Company, Inc.

Front view of the prefabricated bow piece being positioned with a crawler tractor on the JOHN J. BOLAND September 26, 1952.

Wisconsin Maritime Museum & The Manitowoc Company, Inc.

This side view shows the prefabricated bow piece being lined up with the forward bottom plates of the JOHN J. BOLAND September 26, 1952.

Chapter 3: JOHN J. BOLAND III 179

Wisconsin Maritime Museum & The Manitowoc Company, Inc.

View shows the bow in place and the rest of the JOHN J. BOLAND
being constructed up to it October 30, 1952.

Wisconsin Maritime Museum & The Manitowoc Company, Inc.

View of the stern with more upper hull completed and the rudder in
place on the JOHN J. BOLAND October 30, 1952.

Wisconsin Maritime Museum & The Manitowoc Company, Inc.

Bow view of the JOHN J. BOLAND with an upper forward bulkhead
and more hull sides in place on October 30, 1952.

Wisconsin Maritime Museum & The Manitowoc Company, Inc.

Reduction gear that will couple the low pressure, in the foreground, and the high pressure turbines
to the propeller shaft, is being hoisted into place on the JOHN J. BOLAND December 6, 1952.

Wisconsin Maritime Museum & The Manitowoc Company, Inc.
Front view of the full hull of the JOHN J. BOLAND December 6, 1952.

Wisconsin Maritime Museum & The Manitowoc Company, Inc.
View looking forward of the cargo hold that is curving upward for the yet to be installed self-unloading system on the JOHN J. BOLAND December 6, 1952.

Wisconsin Maritime Museum & The Manitowoc Company, Inc.

The cargo hold of the JOHN J. BOLAND showing the self-unloading system center inverted V structure and deck beams being added above, with a cargo hold bulkhead in the background January 1, 1953.

Wisconsin Maritime Museum & The Manitowoc Company, Inc.

View looking forward over the deck showing the hatch openings and the construction crane still in the hold of the nearly completed hull of the JOHN J. BOLAND January 1, 1953.

Chapter 3: JOHN J. BOLAND III 183

Wisconsin Maritime Museum & The Manitowoc Company, Inc.

Front view of the hull of the JOHN J. BOLAND January 1, 1952 with plating in process and the port anchor shoot completed.

Wisconsin Maritime Museum & The Manitowoc Company, Inc.

Stern view with aft deck house being added on the JOHN J. BOLAND January 1, 1953.

Wisconsin Maritime Museum & The Manitowoc Company, Inc.

With some of the construction scaffolding removed, the painted stern of
the JOHN J. BOLAND can now be seen February 13, 1953.

Wisconsin Maritime Museum & The Manitowoc Company, Inc.

View of the bow of the JOHN J. BOLAND showing the completed hull
plating and the deckhouse being fabricated on February 13, 1953.

Chapter 3: JOHN J. BOLAND III

Wisconsin Maritime Museum & The Manitowoc Company, Inc.

View looking forward over the deck showing the more completed forward deckhouse of the JOHN J. BOLAND March 3, 1953.

Wisconsin Maritime Museum & The Manitowoc Company, Inc.

View of the more completed forward upper deck and deckhouse. Scaffolding has been removed from the midsection of the JOHN J. BOLAND March 3, 1953.

Wisconsin Maritime Museum & The Manitowoc Company, Inc.

Looking forward over the deck showing some of the forward hatch covers retracted and the more completed forward deckhouse of the JOHN J. BOLAND April 22, 1953.

Wisconsin Maritime Museum & The Manitowoc Company, Inc.

The hull is nearly completed of the JOHN J. BOLAND with aft and forward deckhouses still under construction April 22, 1953.

Wisconsin Maritime Museum & The Manitowoc Company, Inc.

Bow view of the JOHN J. BOLAND on April 22, 1953.

Wisconsin Maritime Museum & The Manitowoc Company, Inc.
The stack is being hoisted into place on the JOHN J. BOLAND April 25, 1953.

Chapter 3: JOHN J. BOLAND III 189

Wisconsin Maritime Museum & The Manitowoc Company, Inc.

View looking aft over the open deck hatches at the aft deckhouse with
the stack installed on the JOHN J. BOLAND April 15, 1953.

Wisconsin Maritime Museum & The Manitowoc Company, Inc.

The prefabricated pilot house is being readied for hoisting onto the JOHN J. BOLAND April 25, 1953.

Wisconsin Maritime Museum & The Manitowoc Company, Inc.

The pilot house of the JOHN J. BOLAND is being craned into place April 25, 1953.

Launch bunking under the stern of the JOHN J. BOLAND on May 8, 1953.

View underneath the starboard stern showing the propeller shaft tube, the propeller hub, launch bunking and part of the launch trigger mechanism of the JOHN J. BOLAND May 8, 1953.

Wisconsin Maritime Museum & The Manitowoc Company, Inc.

Some of the bunking under the bow of the JOHN J. BOLAND also showing
part of the compressed air piping for the launch line cutters May 8, 1953.

Wisconsin Maritime Museum & The Manitowoc Company, Inc.

Close view of the stern launch trigger under the JOHN J. BOLAND May 8, 1953.

Wisconsin Maritime Museum & The Manitowoc Company, Inc.

Launch bunks and trigger mechanism under the bow of the JOHN J. BOLAND May 8, 1953.

Wisconsin Maritime Museum & The Manitowoc Company, Inc.

View underneath the port stern with markings showing how many men will be required at each station to pound wedges to lift the JOHN J. BOLAND onto the launch skids May 8, 1953.

Wisconsin Maritime Museum & The Manitowoc Company, Inc.

View of the men pounding the wedges to raise the JOHN J. BOLAND
onto the launch skids within an hour of launch May 9, 1953.

Wisconsin Maritime Museum & The Manitowoc Company, Inc.

View from across the river of the JOHN J. BOLAND ready for launch May 9, 1953.

Wisconsin Maritime Museum & The Manitowoc Company, Inc.
Launch of the JOHN J. BOLAND May 9, 1953.

Wisconsin Maritime Museum & The Manitowoc Company, Inc.
View from the yard of the launch of the JOHN J. BOLAND May 9, 1953.

Wisconsin Maritime Museum & The Manitowoc Company, Inc.

The upper self-unloading elevator machinery is under construction on the JOHN J. BOLAND June 17, 1953.

Wisconsin Maritime Museum & The Manitowoc Company, Inc.

Finish work in process on the JOHN J. BOLAND June 17, 1953.

Chapter 3: JOHN J. BOLAND III 197

Wisconsin Maritime Museum & The Manitowoc Company, Inc.

Aft finish work including propeller blade installation on the JOHN J. BOLAND June 17, 1953.

Wisconsin Maritime Museum & The Manitowoc Company, Inc.

The self-unloading boom support frame is being hoisted on the
JOHN J. BOLAND with the boiler crane July 18, 1953.

Wisconsin Maritime Museum & The Manitowoc Company, Inc.

The self-unloading boom support frame is in place and more forward finish work is completed on the JOHN J. BOLAND July 18, 1953.

Wisconsin Maritime Museum & The Manitowoc Company, Inc.

The forward anchor windlass and haws pipes are shown on the JOHN J. BOLAND September 22, 1953.

Wisconsin Maritime Museum & The Manitowoc Company, Inc.
One of the tunnels is shown on the JOHN J. BOLAND September 22, 1953.

Wisconsin Maritime Museum & The Manitowoc Company, Inc.
The boilers controls on the JOHN J. BOLAND September 22, 1953.

Wisconsin Maritime Museum & The Manitowoc Company, Inc.
One of the Foster-Wheeler boilers is shown on the JOHN J. BOLAND September 22, 1953.

Chapter 3: JOHN J. BOLAND III 201

Wisconsin Maritime Museum & The Manitowoc Company, Inc.

The DeLaval high pressure turbine is in the foreground with the low pressure turbine in the background on the JOHN J. BOLAND September 22, 1953.

Wisconsin Maritime Museum & The Manitowoc Company, Inc.

The low pressure DeLaval turbine with part of the reduction gear is shown on the JOHN J. BOLAND September 22, 1953.

Wisconsin Maritime Museum & The Manitowoc Company, Inc.
View of the engine room on the JOHN J. BOLAND September 22, 1953.

Wisconsin Maritime Museum & The Manitowoc Company, Inc.
The engine control panel in the engine room on the JOHN J. BOLAND September 22, 1953.

Wisconsin Maritime Museum & The Manitowoc Company, Inc.

View from overhead of the DeLaval steam turbines and reduction gear on the JOHN J. BOLAND September 22, 1953.

Wisconsin Maritime Museum & The Manitowoc Company, Inc.

The navigation room, aft of the pilot house, with the gyrocompass in the foreground on the JOHN J. BOLAND September 22, 1953.

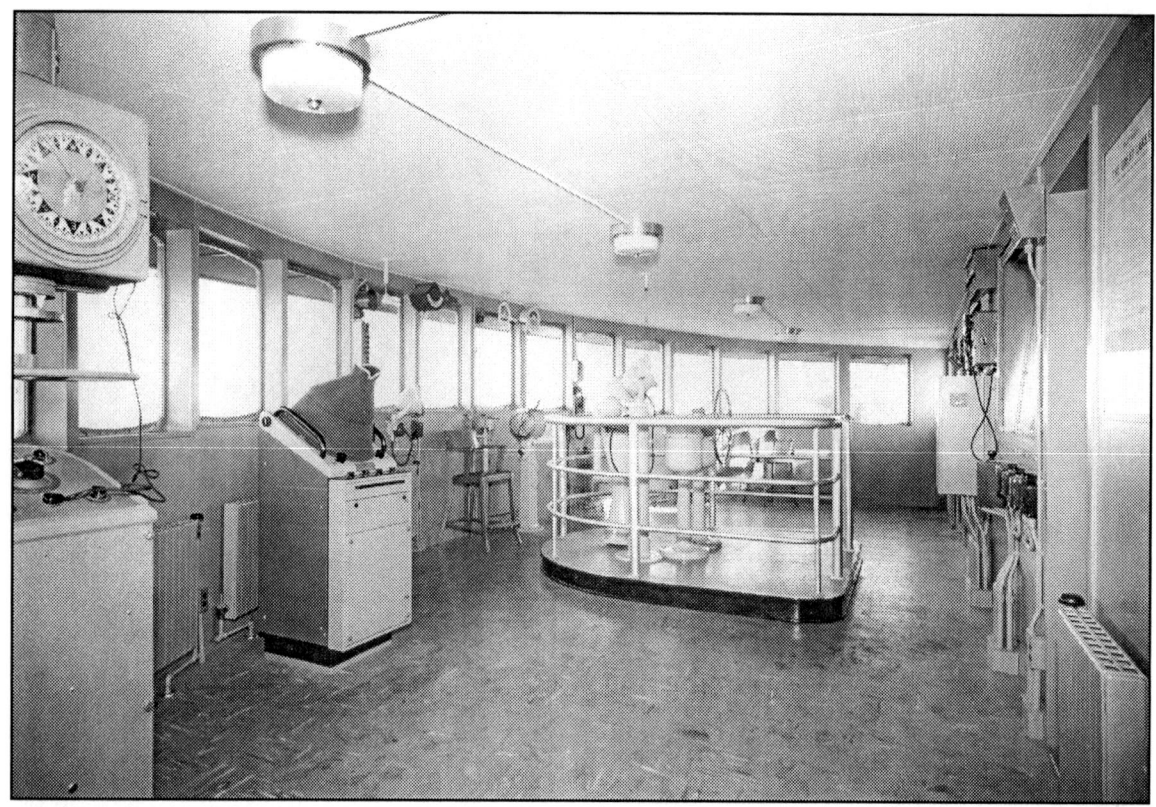

Wisconsin Maritime Museum & The Manitowoc Company, Inc.
View of the pilot house looking to starboard of the JOHN J. BOLAND September 22, 1953.

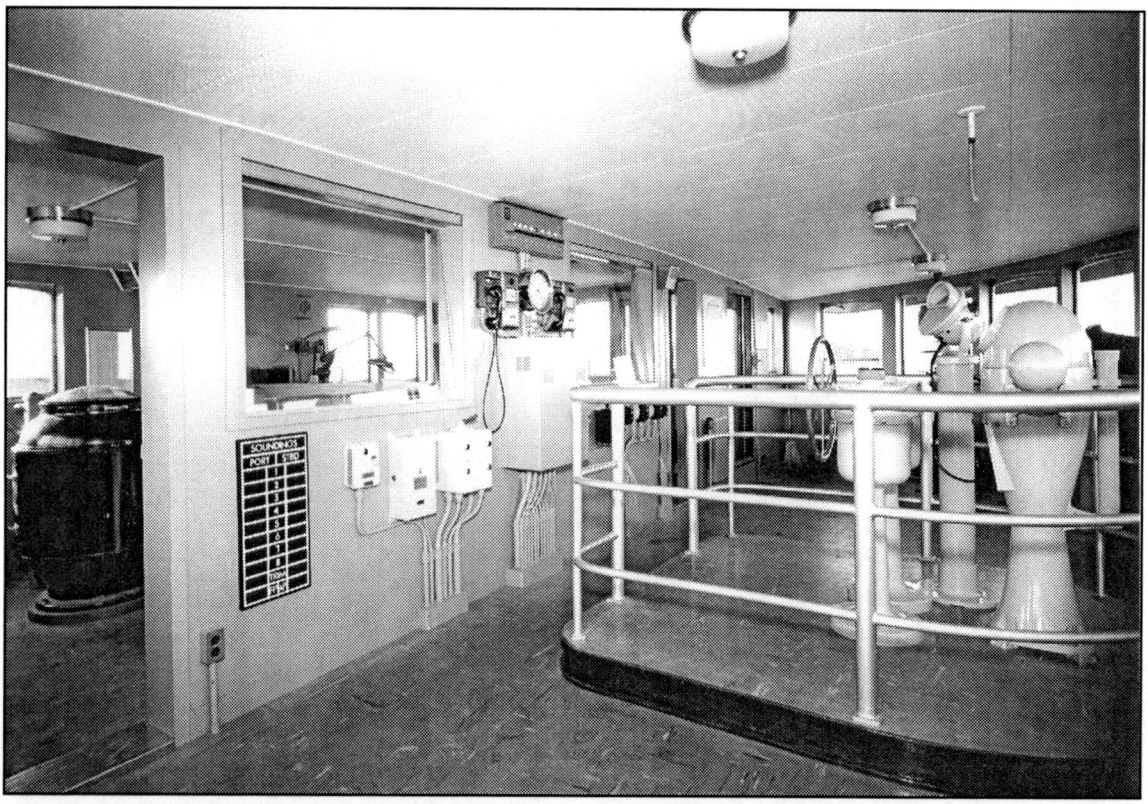

Wisconsin Maritime Museum & The Manitowoc Company, Inc.
The helm is shown on the JOHN J. BOLAND September 22, 1953.

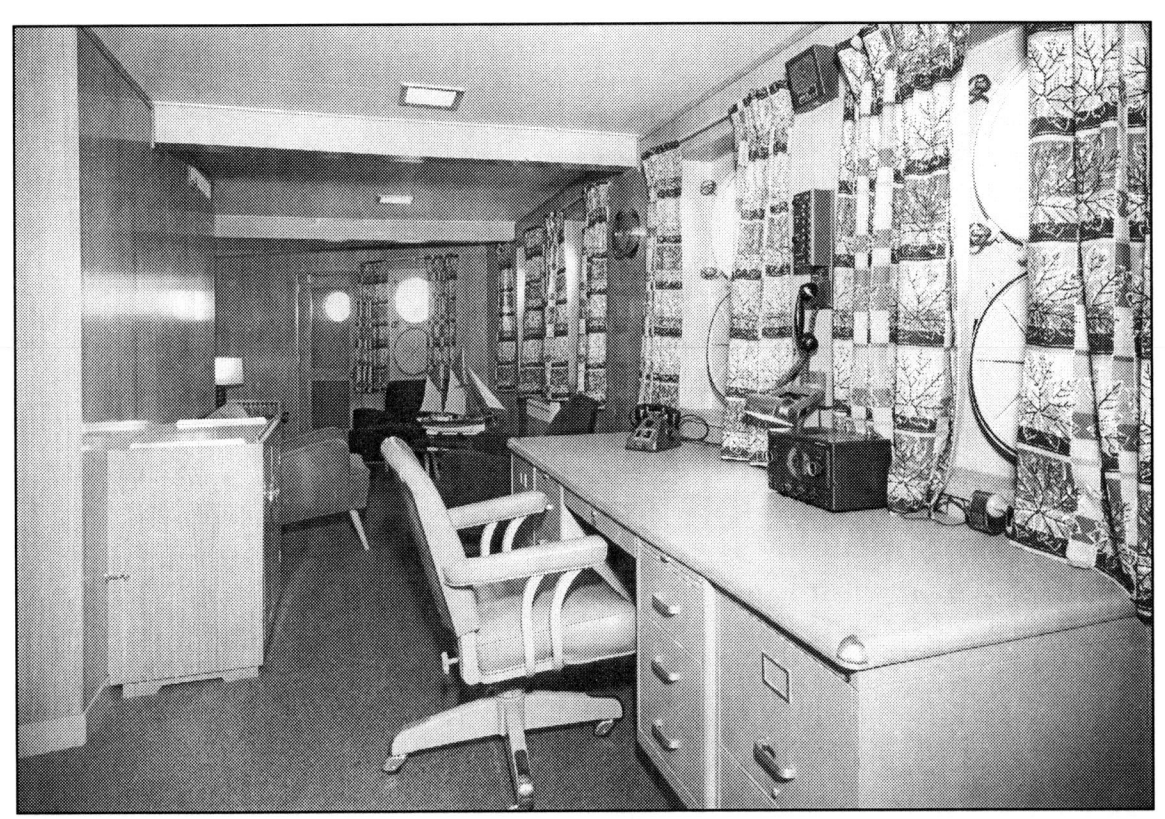

Chapter 3: JOHN J. BOLAND III

Wisconsin Maritime Museum & The Manitowoc Company, Inc.

The captain's office on the JOHN J. BOLAND September 22, 1953.

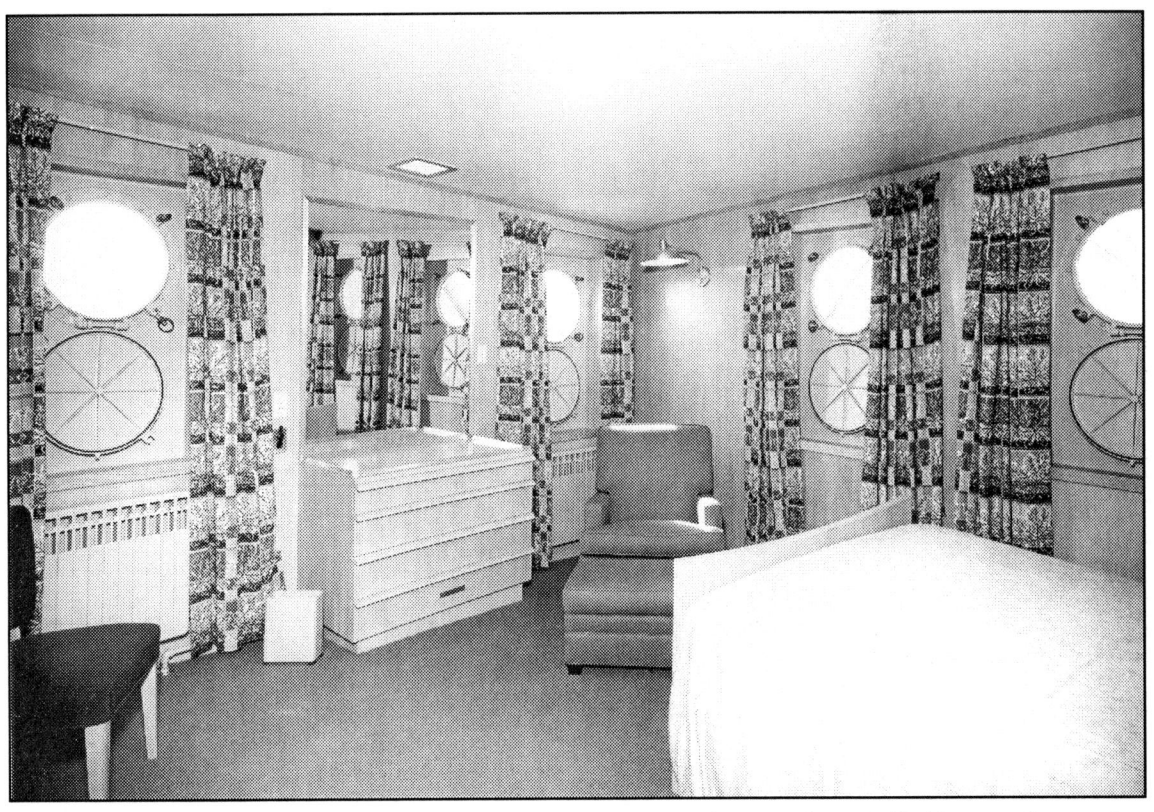

Wisconsin Maritime Museum & The Manitowoc Company, Inc.

The captain's quarters on the JOHN J. BOLAND September 22, 1953.

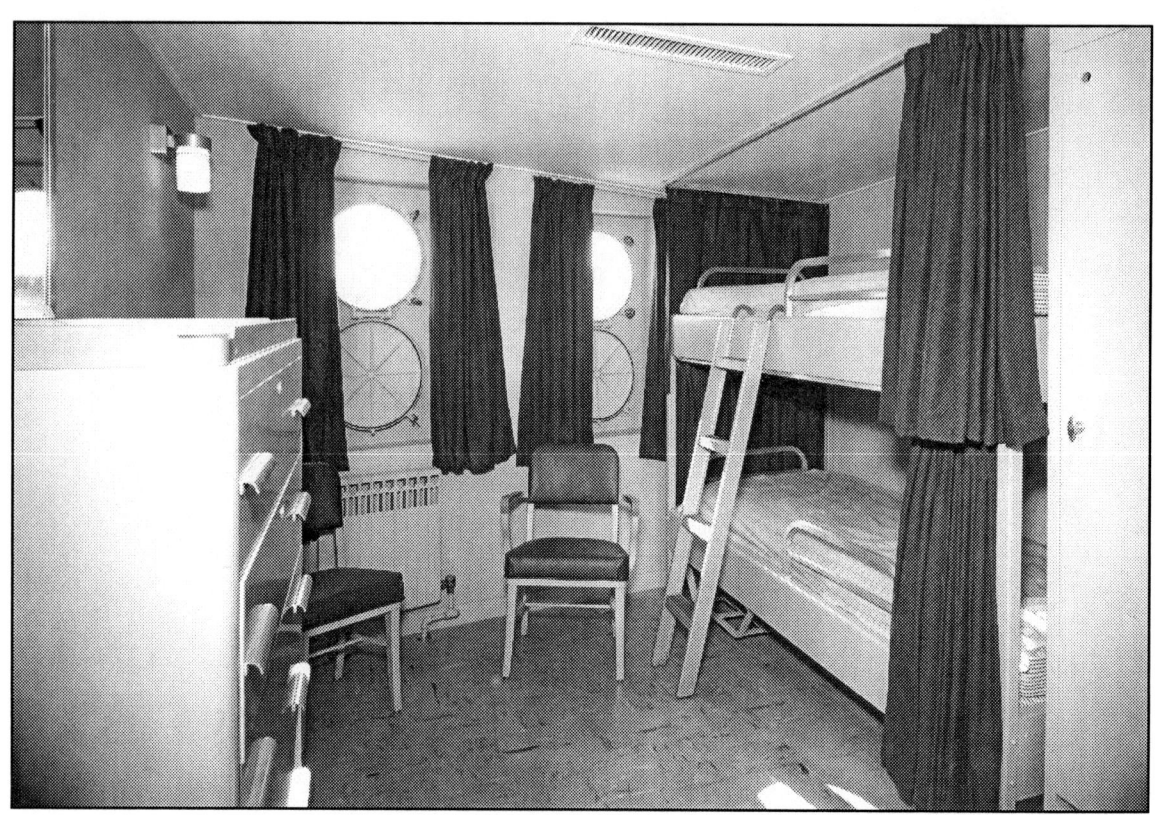

Wisconsin Maritime Museum & The Manitowoc Company, Inc.
Typical crew's quarters on the JOHN J. BOLAND September 22, 1953.

Wisconsin Maritime Museum & The Manitowoc Company, Inc.
View of the galley of the JOHN J. BOLAND September 22, 1953.

Wisconsin Maritime Museum & The Manitowoc Company, Inc.
The guests' dinning room is shown on the JOHN J. BOLAND September 22, 1953.

Wisconsin Maritime Museum & The Manitowoc Company, Inc.
The officers' dinning room on the JOHN J. BOLAND September 22, 1953.

Wisconsin Maritime Museum & The Manitowoc Company, Inc.
Crew's dinning room on the JOHN J. BOLAND September 22, 1953.

Wisconsin Maritime Museum & The Manitowoc Company, Inc.
The self-unloading boom is under test on the JOHN J. BOLAND down the Manitowoc River from the yard, just upstream from the grain elevator September 22, 1953.

Stern view of the JOHN J. BOLAND tied along the Manitowoc River for testing September 22, 1953.

The JOHN J. BOLAND is passing down the Manitowoc River
through the Eight Street Bridge September 22, 1953.

Wisconsin Maritime Museum & The Manitowoc Company, Inc.
View from the stern of the JOHN J. BOLAND looking forward at the completed self-unloading machinery. The Manitowoc breakwaters and Lake Michigan are in the background September 22, 1953.

Chapter 3: JOHN J. BOLAND III 211

Wisconsin Maritime Museum & The Manitowoc Company, Inc.

View looking aft over the self-unloading boom and the aft deck house on the JOHN J. BOLAND, with the Eighth Street Bridge over the Manitowoc River in the background September 22, 1953.

Wisconsin Maritime Museum & The Manitowoc Company, Inc.

View of the completed forward self-unloading structure and forward deck house of the JOHN J. BOLAND September 22, 1953.

Wisconsin Maritime Museum & The Manitowoc Company, Inc.

The JOHN J. BOLAND is shown on sea trials in Lake Michigan September 22, 1953.

Wisconsin Maritime Museum & The Manitowoc Company, Inc.

Parting shot September 23, 1953.

Chapter 4

DETROIT EDISON II

DETROIT EDISON II 1955 Hull # 418   Official No. 269187

Detroit Edison was the major electric power utility in the greater Detroit area. The American Steamship Company recognized the utility as one of its largest customers by naming this vessel the DETROIT EDISON.

Manitowoc Shipbuilding, Inc., Manitowoc, Wisconsin
    Customer – American Steamship Company
    Designer – Manitowoc Shipbuilding Company
    Plans and specifications – Steel self-unloader – length 606 feet – length between perpendiculars 590 feet – length of keel 580 feet – beam 72 feet – depth – 38.5 feet – draft 26.5 feet – gross tons 12,172 – net tons 8,744 – cargo capacity 20,000 tons limestone or 16,500 tons coal – self-unloading boom length 250 feet – unloading rates – 2500 tons per hour coal and 4500 tons per hour limestone – hatches, 27 on 12 foot centers, 45 feet 6 inches wide X 9 feet long – 6 cargo holds – service speed 16.25 miles per hour – total crew 41 – cost $6,700,000 –
    Engine – DeLaval steam cross compound turbine – double reduction gear – 7,700 horsepower maximum – 7,000 horsepower normal
    Boilers – Two Foster-Wheeler – water tube
    Propeller – 4 blade
    Fuel – coal
    Construction
        Keel laid – July 28, 1953
        Launch – September 9, 1954
        Sea trials – April 14, 1955
        Commissioned – April 15, 1955
        Delivered – April 15, 1955
    Log – The DETROIT EDISON sailed April 15, 1955 for Port Inland, Michigan to take on a load of limestone for Indiana Harbor.
        Lengthened to 678 feet – length between perpendiculars 662 feet – gross tons 13,723 – net tons 10,296 – hatches, 33 on 12 foot centers, 45 feet 6 inches wide X 9 feet long – 7 cargo holds Fraser Shipyard, Superior, Wisconsin 1965 and 1966
        Converted to fuel oil with 105,000 gallons capacity 1971
        Grounded on Gray's Reef, Lake Michigan December 22, 1980 – repaired Bay Shipbuilding, Sturgeon Bay, Wisconsin
        Laid up 1984 through 1986
    Final status – Scrapped Goldwils Inc., Brownsville, TX 1987

Wisconsin Maritime Museum & The Manitowoc Company, Inc.

The propeller shaft bearing, rudder stock and fairing are being fabricated for the DETROIT EDISON June 17, 1953.

Wisconsin Maritime Museum & The Manitowoc Company, Inc.

Keel blocks with the first keel plates along side for the DETROIT EDISON July 28, 1953.

Chapter 4: DETROIT EDISON II 217

Wisconsin Maritime Museum & The Manitowoc Company, Inc.

Keel laying and welding the first two keel pieces for the DETROIT EDISON July 28, 1953.

Wisconsin Maritime Museum & The Manitowoc Company, Inc.

Fabricating stern piece frames of the DETROIT EDISON July 28, 1953.

Wisconsin Maritime Museum & The Manitowoc Company, Inc.

View showing the stern double bottom sections of the DETROIT EDISON with
the nearly completed JOHN J. BOLAND along side August 21, 1953.

Wisconsin Maritime Museum & The Manitowoc Company, Inc.

Bottom plating is being fabricated in front of the stern double bottom
piece of the DETROIT EDISON September 9, 1953.

Chapter 4: DETROIT EDISON II 219

Wisconsin Maritime Museum & The Manitowoc Company, Inc.

Plates are being fit and welded to the stern piece of the DETROIT EDISON September 11, 1953.

Wisconsin Maritime Museum & The Manitowoc Company, Inc.

The stern piece for the DETROIT EDISON is being positioned with Speedcranes September 19, 1953.

Chapter 4: DETROIT EDISON II 221

Wisconsin Maritime Museum & The Manitowoc Company, Inc.

View from the stern of the DETROIT EDISON showing the stern piece,
stern frames and the port aft side tank October 3, 1953.

Wisconsin Maritime Museum & The Manitowoc Company, Inc.

Stern side and lower deck frames have been prefabricated for
the DETROIT EDISON October 3, 1953.

Wisconsin Maritime Museum & The Manitowoc Company, Inc.

View looking straight aft on centerline of the keel of the DETROIT EDISON October 3, 1953.

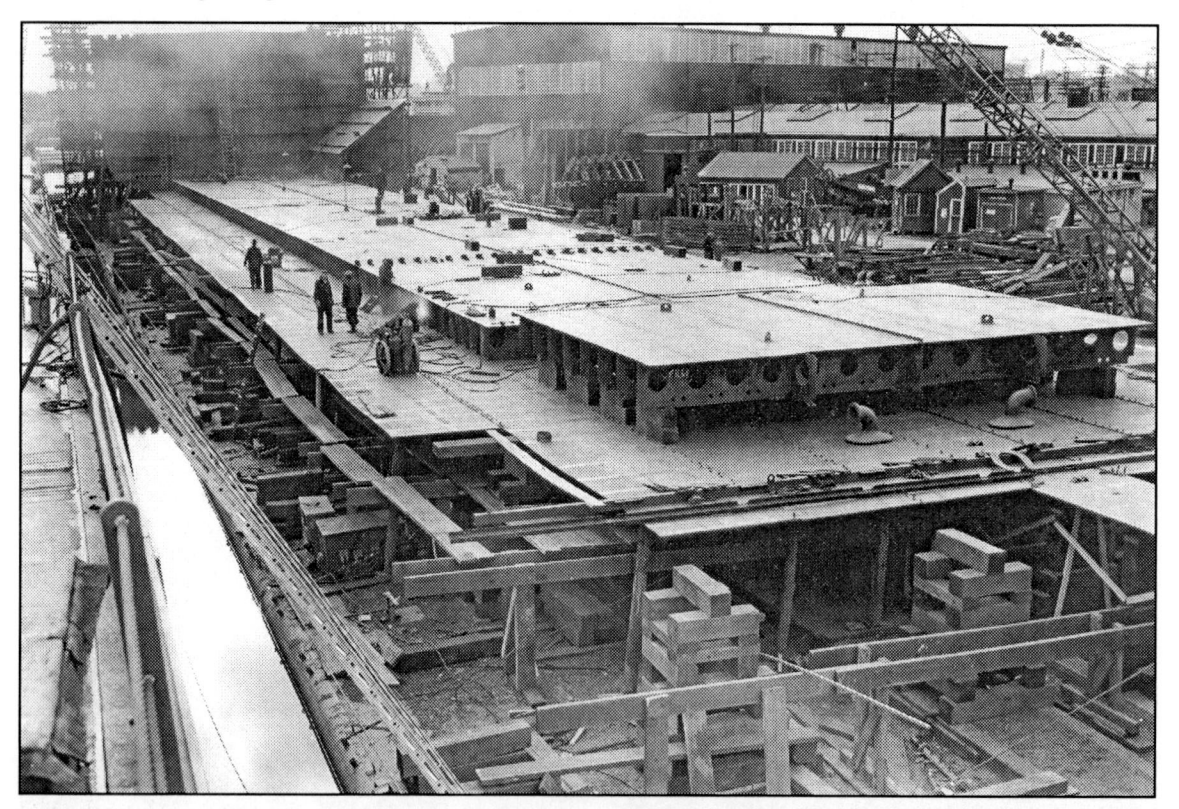

Wisconsin Maritime Museum & The Manitowoc Company, Inc.

Double bottom sections are being welded in place with aft bottom and side sections
and a rear bulkhead in place on the DETROIT EDISON November 27, 1953.

Chapter 4: DETROIT EDISON II 223

Wisconsin Maritime Museum & The Manitowoc Company, Inc.

View from the stern of the DETROIT EDISON November 27, 1953.

Wisconsin Maritime Museum & The Manitowoc Company, Inc.

Upper stern framing is being added on the DETROIT EDISON December 21, 1953.

Wisconsin Maritime Museum & The Manitowoc Company, Inc.

Bow bottom frames with a more complete stern in the background
of the DETROIT EDISON December 21, 1953.

Wisconsin Maritime Museum & The Manitowoc Company, Inc.

Plating is being fit and welded to the bow of the DETROIT EDISON January 22, 1954.

Chapter 4: DETROIT EDISON II

Wisconsin Maritime Museum & The Manitowoc Company, Inc.

Inside of the cargo hold of the DETROIT EDISON with the bottom,
sides and aft deck beams in place January 22, 1953.

Wisconsin Maritime Museum & The Manitowoc Company, Inc.

Bow section and forward bulkhead in place as viewed from inside
the DETROIT EDISON February 26, 1954.

Wisconsin Maritime Museum & The Manitowoc Company, Inc.

Looking aft showing more bottom and side sections, upper side sections and deck beams on the DETROIT EDISON February 26, 1954.

Wisconsin Maritime Museum & The Manitowoc Company, Inc.

Bow piece in place with sections and framing advancing toward the bow of the DETROIT EDISON March 21, 1954.

Wisconsin Maritime Museum & The Manitowoc Company, Inc.

View from the bow of the DETROIT EDISON shrouded in construction scaffolding April 17, 1954.

Wisconsin Maritime Museum & The Manitowoc Company, Inc.

View from the stern of the DETROIT EDISON with the rudder in place April 17, 1954.

Wisconsin Maritime Museum & The Manitowoc Company, Inc.

Looking forward on the deck of the DETROIT EDISON
showing the cargo hold deck beams April 17, 1954.

Wisconsin Maritime Museum & The Manitowoc Company, Inc.

Cargo hold hatch covers on the DETROIT EDISON May 16, 1954.

Chapter 4: DETROIT EDISON II

Wisconsin Maritime Museum & The Manitowoc Company, Inc.

Bow view of the DETROIT EDISON May 16, 1954.

Wisconsin Maritime Museum & The Manitowoc Company, Inc.

View from the stern showing construction beginning on the aft deck house of the DETROIT EDISON May 16, 1954.

230 Freighters of Manitowoc

Wisconsin Maritime Museum & The Manitowoc Company, Inc.
Looking forward with deck hatches in the foreground and the self-unloading elevator under construction on the DETROIT EDISON June 20, 1954.

Wisconsin Maritime Museum & The Manitowoc Company, Inc.
View of the bow with the shell plating completed on the DETROIT EDISON June 20, 1954.

Chapter 4: DETROIT EDISON II 231

Wisconsin Maritime Museum & The Manitowoc Company, Inc.

Stern view with some scaffolding removed, more aft deck house completed and painting in process on the DETROIT EDISON June 20, 1954.

Wisconsin Maritime Museum & The Manitowoc Company, Inc.

View from across the river of the DETROIT EDISON hull nearing completion June 20, 1954.

Wisconsin Maritime Museum & The Manitowoc Company, Inc.

Looking forward, this view shows the deck hatches, the self-unloading elevator and the forward deck house of the DETROIT EDISON August 7, 1954.

Wisconsin Maritime Museum & The Manitowoc Company, Inc.

Looking over the deck hatches with the aft deck house and stack in the background on the DETROIT EDISON August 7, 1954.

Chapter 4: DETROIT EDISON II

Wisconsin Maritime Museum & The Manitowoc Company, Inc.

The bow of the DETROIT EDISON is shown with the forward deck house and pilot house in place and bottom painting complete August 7, 1954.

Wisconsin Maritime Museum & The Manitowoc Company, Inc.

The DETROIT EDISON is nearing completion for launch August 7, 1954.

Wisconsin Maritime Museum & The Manitowoc Company, Inc.
View from the river showing the DETROIT EDISON on the ways August 12, 1954.

Wisconsin Maritime Museum & The Manitowoc Company, Inc.
Bow view of the DETROIT EDISON christening stand and launch preparations September 9, 1954.

Chapter 4: DETROIT EDISON II 235

Wisconsin Maritime Museum & The Manitowoc Company, Inc.

View of the men pounding the wedges to raise the DETROIT EDISON onto
the launch skids less than an hour from launch September 9, 1954.

Wisconsin Maritime Museum & The Manitowoc Company, Inc.

The DETROIT EDISON on her way into the water with the launch party
on the christening stand in the foreground September 9, 1954.

Wisconsin Maritime Museum & The Manitowoc Company, Inc.
View from across the river of the launch of the DETROIT EDISON September 9, 1954.

Wisconsin Maritime Museum & The Manitowoc Company, Inc.
Yard side view of the launch of the DETROIT EDISON September 9, 1954.

Chapter 4: DETROIT EDISON II 237

Wisconsin Maritime Museum & The Manitowoc Company, Inc.

After the launch, the bow and stern hausers are pulling the DETROIT EDISON back to the dock September 9, 1954.

Wisconsin Maritime Museum & The Manitowoc Company, Inc.

View looking aft from aft of the pilot house at the self-unloading boom support frame, elevator and boom of the DETROIT EDISON April 14, 1955.

The pilot house of the DETROIT EDISON is shown looking to port April 14, 1955.

This view is looking aft from the pilot house into the navigation room of the DETROIT EDISON April 14, 1955.

Wisconsin Maritime Museum & The Manitowoc Company, Inc.
The captain's quarters on the DETROIT EDISON April 14, 1955.

Wisconsin Maritime Museum & The Manitowoc Company, Inc.
The captain's office on the DETROIT EDISON April 14, 1955.

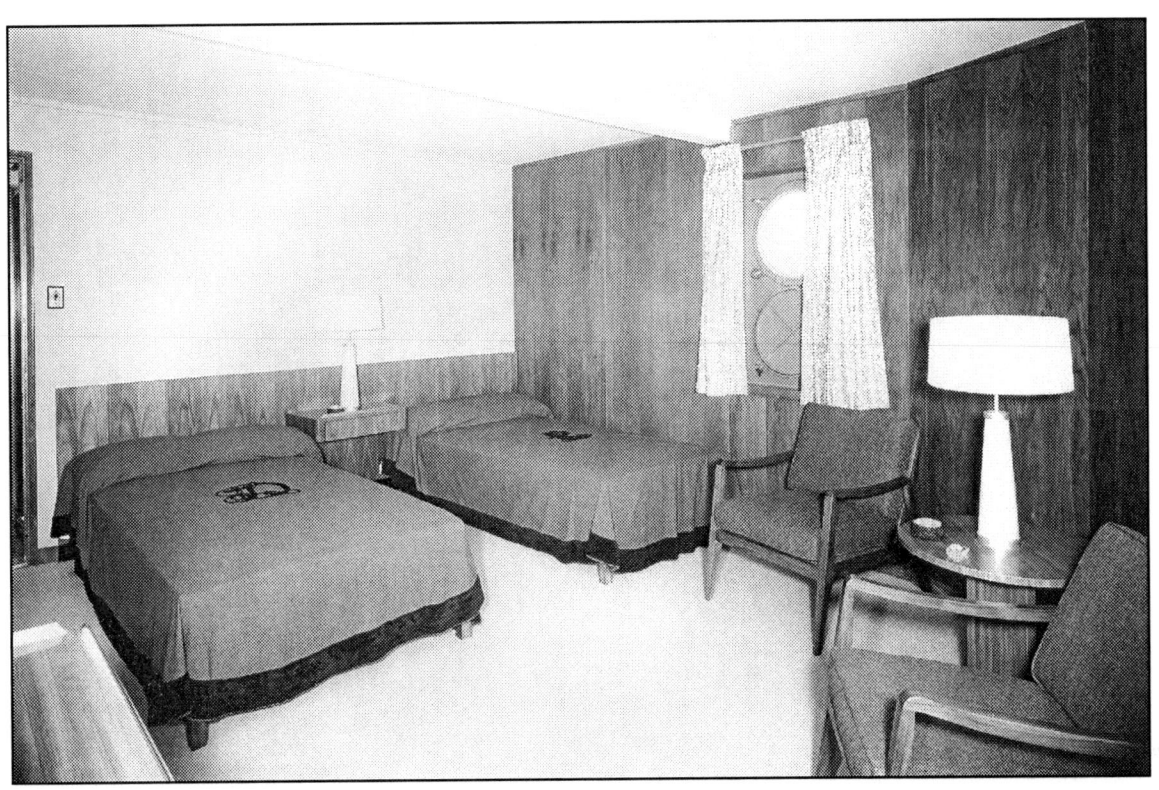

Wisconsin Maritime Museum & The Manitowoc Company, Inc.
Guest quarters on the DETROIT EDISON April 14, 1955.

Wisconsin Maritime Museum & The Manitowoc Company, Inc.
Guest lounge of the DETROIT EDISON April 14, 1955.

Wisconsin Maritime Museum & The Manitowoc Company, Inc.
Officers' dining room on the DETROIT EDISON April 14, 1955.

Wisconsin Maritime Museum & The Manitowoc Company, Inc.
Crew's dining room on the DETROIT EDISON April 14, 1955.

Chapter 4: DETROIT EDISON II 243

Wisconsin Maritime Museum & The Manitowoc Company, Inc.

View of the engine room of the DETROIT EDISON April 14, 1955.

Wisconsin Maritime Museum & The Manitowoc Company, Inc.

The DeLaval low pressure turbine is shown on the left with the high pressure turbine on the right in the DETROIT EDISON April 14, 1955.

Wisconsin Maritime Museum & The Manitowoc Company, Inc.
The engine control room of the DETROIT EDISON April 14, 1955.

Wisconsin Maritime Museum & The Manitowoc Company, Inc.
The boiler stokers on the DETROIT EDISON April 14, 1955.

Chapter 4: DETROIT EDISON II

Wisconsin Maritime Museum & The Manitowoc Company, Inc.
View down one of the tunnels on the DETROIT EDISON April 14, 1955.

Wisconsin Maritime Museum & The Manitowoc Company, Inc.
The electromechanical steering gear on the DETROIT EDISON April 14, 1955.

Wisconsin Maritime Museum & The Manitowoc Company, Inc.
The rudder shaft of the DETROIT EDISON April 14, 1955.

Wisconsin Maritime Museum & The Manitowoc Company, Inc.
The DETROIT EDISON on sea trials in Lake Michigan April 14, 1955.

Chapter 4: DETROIT EDISON II

Wisconsin Maritime Museum & The Manitowoc Company, Inc.

The DETROIT EDISON tied in the Manitowoc River next to the Rahr Elevator April 14, 1955.

Wisconsin Maritime Museum & The Manitowoc Company, Inc.

Parting shot April 15, 1955.

Charles C. West died October 3, 1957. John D. West became President of the Manitowoc Company 1957.

John D. West was the son of company co-founder Charles C. West and born May 24, 1906 in Manitowoc, Wisconsin. He earned a Bachelor of Science Degree in Mechanical Engineering from Cornell University in 1932 and was instrumental in the successful construction of the 28 submarines. He was known for his engineering skills and his inventiveness.

The Manitowoc Company, Inc.

John D. West

Chapter 5

ADAM E. CORNELIUS III

ADAM E. CORNELIUS III 1959 Hull # 424　　　　　Official No. 278853

    Mr. Adam Edward Cornelius was born June 25, 1882 in Buffalo, New York. In 1901, after high school graduation, he began working as a clerk and stenographer in a vessel brokerage office. In 1904 he co-founded the vessel operation and brokerage firm of Boland and Cornelius. In 1907 the firm became the American Steamship Company. Mr. Cornelius became chairman of the board of the firm in 1915 and remained in that position until he died December 10, 1953. Mr. Cornelius was also a major influence in the expansion of the self-unloading vessels on the Great Lakes.

  Manitowoc Shipbuilding, Inc., Manitowoc, Wisconsin
      Customer – American Steamship Company
      Plans and specifications – Steel self-unloader – length 666 feet – length between perpendiculars 650 feet – length of keel 640 feet – beam 72 feet – depth 40 feet – draft 27 feet – gross tons 14,084 – net tons 8,915 – cargo capacity 23,800 tons limestone or 19,500 tons coal – forward boom length 250 feet – unloading rates – 3100 tons per hour coal and 5600 tons per hour limestone – hatches, 17 on 24 foot centers, 45 feet 6 inches wide X 12 feet long – 6 cargo holds – service speed 16.6 miles per hour – total crew 42 – cost $7,200,000
      Engine – DeLaval steam cross compound turbine – double reduction gear – 7,700 horsepower maximum – 7,000 horsepower normal @110 revolutions per minute
      Boilers – Two Foster-Wheeler – water tube
      Propeller – 17.5 feet diameter – 4 blade – steel
      Fuel – coal – capacity 700 tons
      Construction
          Keel laid – October 25, 1957
          Launch – November 25, 1958
          Sea trials – June 4, 1959
          Commissioned – June 6, 1959
          Delivered – June 6, 1959
      Log – Converted to oil by 1972
          Bow plates damaged in ice and current – Muamee River, Toledo, Ohio January 19, 1975
          Machinery damage Lake Huron May 22, 1978
          Laid up Toledo, Ohio 1985 through 1988
          Sold to Marine Salvage of Port Colbourne, Ontario 1988
          Converted to a sea going barge – length 594 feet in Halifax, Nova Scotia for Keybulk Transportation – renamed CAPTAIN EDWARD V. SMITH in 1989
          Sold to Halifax Grain Elevator LTD division of Great Lakes Transport LTD. – renamed SEA BARGE ONE in 1991
          Laid up 1994
          Renamed – SARAH SPENCER in 2001
      Current status – in service for Halifax Grain Elevator LTD division of Great Lakes Transport LTD

Wisconsin Maritime Museum & The Manitowoc Company, Inc.
Keel laying for the ADAM E. CORNELIUS October 15, 1957.

Wisconsin Maritime Museum & The Manitowoc Company, Inc.
The first two plates of the ADAM E. CORNELIUS are in
position on the keel blocks October 15, 1957.

Chapter 5: ADAM E. CORNELIUS III

Wisconsin Maritime Museum & The Manitowoc Company, Inc.

Laying some of the first double bottom sections of the ADAM E. CORNELIUS November 15, 1957.

Wisconsin Maritime Museum & The Manitowoc Company, Inc.

Bottom plates toward the bow are shown with double bottom pieces in place in the background of ADAM E. CORNELIUS November 15, 1957.

Wisconsin Maritime Museum & The Manitowoc Company, Inc.

More bottom plates and double bottom sections are shown with a Manitowoc Speedcrane on the double bottom of the ADAM E. CORNELIUS December 15, 1957.

Wisconsin Maritime Museum & The Manitowoc Company, Inc.

First port and starboard double bottom and side sections are shown in the background of the ADAM E. CORNELIUS January 15, 1958.

Chapter 5: ADAM E. CORNELIUS III 253

Wisconsin Maritime Museum & The Manitowoc Company, Inc.

View from the stern looking forward of the double bottom and side
sections on the ADAM E. CORNELIUS January 15, 1958.

Wisconsin Maritime Museum & The Manitowoc Company, Inc.

More double bottom and side sections and the first stern double bottom piece are
in place on the ADAM E. CORNELIUS February 15, 1958. The next stern double
bottom piece is in the foreground, the propeller shaft and rudder bearing casting
is in the lower left and several prefabricated side sections are to the right.

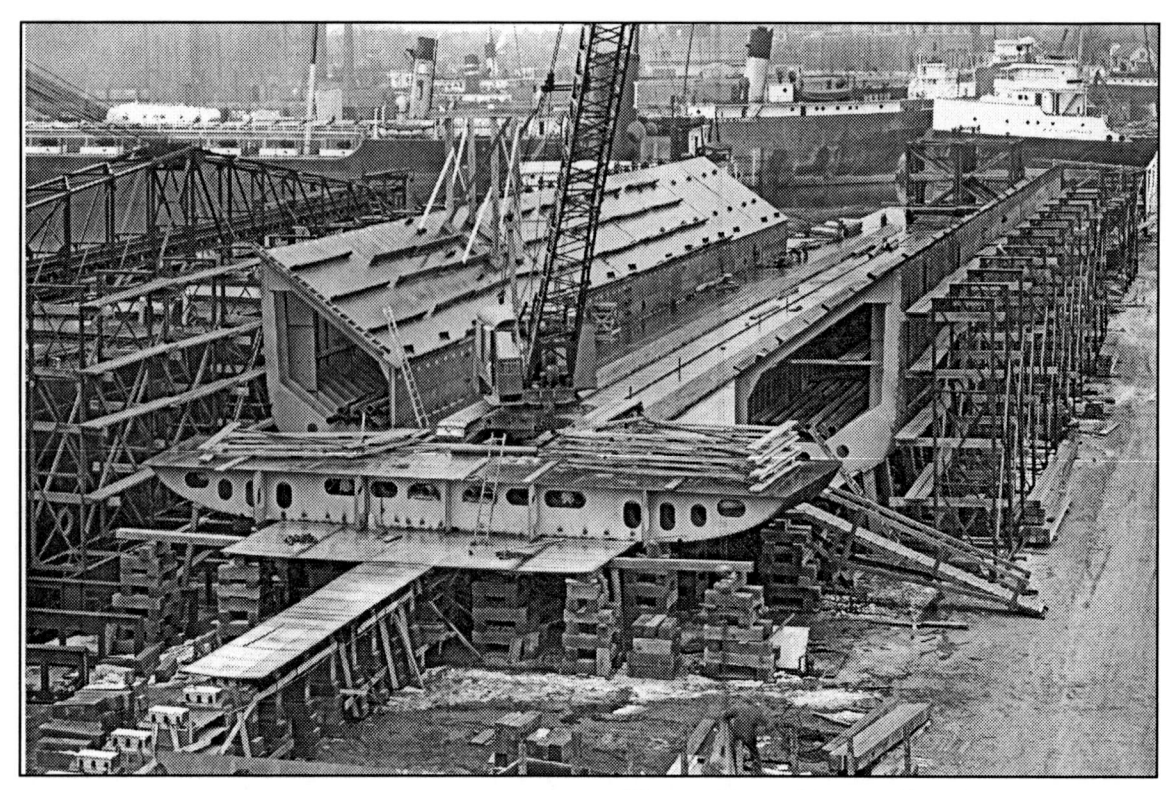

Wisconsin Maritime Museum & The Manitowoc Company, Inc.

The first upper side piece is in place to the left of the crane on
the ADAM E. CORNELIUS March 16, 1958.

Wisconsin Maritime Museum & The Manitowoc Company, Inc.

More stern bottom and upper side pieces are in place on the ADAM E. CORNELIUS April 15, 1958.

Wisconsin Maritime Museum & The Manitowoc Company, Inc.

First bow double bottom piece in place looking aft on the ADAM E. CORNELIUS May 15, 1958.

Wisconsin Maritime Museum & The Manitowoc Company, Inc.

The stern of the ADAM E. CORNELIUS taking shape with upper side plates, aft ballast tanks, more lower stern sections and the propeller shaft bearing and rudder stock casting piece in place May 15, 1958.

Wisconsin Maritime Museum & The Manitowoc Company, Inc.

Upper stern frames and plating with upper sides and the first deck beams in place in the background on the ADAM E. CORNELIUS June 16, 1958.

Wisconsin Maritime Museum & The Manitowoc Company, Inc.

View from the bow showing the narrowing double bottom sections, two prefabricated lower side frames not yet in place and forward cargo hold curving upward of the ADAM E. CORNELIUS June 16, 1958.

Chapter 5: ADAM E. CORNELIUS III

Wisconsin Maritime Museum & The Manitowoc Company, Inc.

More lower bow frames and plating along with forward cargo hold upward curving frames for the self-unloading system on the ADAM E. CORNELIUS July 15, 1958.

Wisconsin Maritime Museum & The Manitowoc Company, Inc.

View from across the Manitowoc River showing the completed mid-body on the ADAM E. CORNELIUS September 15, 1958.

Bow view from across the Manitowoc River showing the completed mid-body and
the forward bulkhead of the ADAM E. CORNELIUS September 15, 1958.

View from across the Manitowoc River showing the nearly completed
stern of the ADAM E. CORNELIUS October 15, 1958.

Wisconsin Maritime Museum & The Manitowoc Company, Inc.

Concentrated effort is being placed on the bow framing and plating on the ADAM E. CORNELIUS to catch up with the nearly completed stern October 15, 1958.

Wisconsin Maritime Museum & The Manitowoc Company, Inc.

The rudder is being installed on the nearly completed ADAM E. CORNELIUS hull with many of the launch skids and bunks in place November 15, 1958.

Wisconsin Maritime Museum & The Manitowoc Company, Inc.

Early launch day showing the bow launching mechanisms and the launch party stand in front of the ADAM E. CORNELIUS in the lower right November 25, 1958.

Wisconsin Maritime Museum & The Manitowoc Company, Inc.

Launch day showing the stern launching mechanisms. The personnel scaffold is still in place to provide access to the deck of the ADAM E. CORNELIUS November 25, 1958.

Chapter 5: ADAM E. CORNELIUS III 261

Wisconsin Maritime Museum & The Manitowoc Company, Inc.

The ADAM E. CORNELIUS in final preparation for launch with the
Reiss tug Green Bay ready to assist November 25, 1958.

Wisconsin Maritime Museum & The Manitowoc Company, Inc.

The launch party on the stand at the bow of the ADAM E. CORNELIUS,
with the Manitowoc Marine Band in the foreground and all launch personnel
at their positions moments before launch November 25, 1958.

Wisconsin Maritime Museum & The Manitowoc Company, Inc.

View from the yard of the launch of the ADAM E. CORNELIUS November 25, 1958.

Wisconsin Maritime Museum & The Manitowoc Company, Inc.

Launch of the ADAM E. CORNELIUS November 25, 1958.

Chapter 5: ADAM E. CORNELIUS III

Wisconsin Maritime Museum & The Manitowoc Company, Inc.

Bow view of the launch of the ADAM E. CORNELIUS November 25, 1958.

Wisconsin Maritime Museum & The Manitowoc Company, Inc.

Seconds after the launch of the ADAM E. CORNELIUS, the wave is
still heading toward the far shore November 28, 1958.

Wisconsin Maritime Museum & The Manitowoc Company, Inc.

Seconds after the launch, the river is full of launching timbers and bunks while the stern line is ready to pull the ADAM E. CORNELIUS back to the dock November 25, 1958.

Wisconsin Maritime Museum & The Manitowoc Company, Inc.

Minutes after launch with the launch party still on the stand, yard workers head down the ways to begin removal of launch debris so the ADAM E. CORNELIUS can be brought dockside November 25, 1958.

Chapter 5: ADAM E. CORNELIUS III 265

Wisconsin Maritime Museum & The Manitowoc Company, Inc.

Hatch covers of the ADAM E. CORNELIUS with the beginning of
the aft deckhouse in the background December 15, 1958.

Wisconsin Maritime Museum & The Manitowoc Company, Inc.

Aft deck house construction on the ADAM E. CORNELIUS December 15, 1958.

Wisconsin Maritime Museum & The Manitowoc Company, Inc.
Bow plating being fit and welded to the ADAM E. CORNELIUS January 15, 1959.

Wisconsin Maritime Museum & The Manitowoc Company, Inc.
Further aft deck house construction of the ADAM E. CORNELIUS January 15, 1959.

Wisconsin Maritime Museum & The Manitowoc Company, Inc.

The forward deck house is under construction on the ADAM E. CORNELIUS February 16, 1959.

Wisconsin Maritime Museum & The Manitowoc Company, Inc.

More aft deck house completed with self-unloading elevator construction just aft of the forward deckhouse on the ADAM E. CORNELIUS February 16, 1959.

Wisconsin Maritime Museum & The Manitowoc Company, Inc.

The forward deck house, pilot house and self-unloading boom support frame
are in place on the ADAM E. CORNELIUS March 19, 1959.

Wisconsin Maritime Museum & The Manitowoc Company, Inc.

Aft deck house construction with smoke stack piping installed
on the ADAM E. CORNELIUS March 19, 1959.

Chapter 5: ADAM E. CORNELIUS III

Wisconsin Maritime Museum & The Manitowoc Company, Inc.

The low pressure turbine and reduction gear in the engine room
of the ADAM E. CORNELIUS March 19, 1959.

Wisconsin Maritime Museum & The Manitowoc Company, Inc.

The self-unloading boom in place as well as the aft deck house with the stack
and aft mast on the ADAM E. CORNELIUS April 16, 1959.

Wisconsin Maritime Museum & The Manitowoc Company, Inc.
Paint work in process on the ADAM E. CORNELIUS May 15, 1959.

Wisconsin Maritime Museum & The Manitowoc Company, Inc.
Boiler, engine and generator being test run on the ADAM E. CORNELIUS May 15, 1959.

Chapter 5: ADAM E. CORNELIUS III 271

Wisconsin Maritime Museum & The Manitowoc Company, Inc.
Bow view of the ADAM E. CORNELIUS on sea trials on Lake Michigan June 4, 1959.

Wisconsin Maritime Museum & The Manitowoc Company, Inc.
View from aft of the ADAM E. CORNELIUS on sea trials in Lake
Michigan during an emergency stop maneuver June 4, 1959.

Wisconsin Maritime Museum & The Manitowoc Company, Inc.

The reduction gear is shown in the ADAM E. CORNELIUS with the low pressure turbine in foreground and the high pressure turbine in background June 6, 1959.

Wisconsin Maritime Museum & The Manitowoc Company, Inc.

The DeLaval steam turbine engine is shown in the ADAM E. CORNELIUS with the low pressure turbine on the left and the high pressure turbine on the right June 6, 1959.

Wisconsin Maritime Museum & The Manitowoc Company, Inc.

The engine control room on the ADAM E. CORNELIUS June 6, 1959.

Wisconsin Maritime Museum & The Manitowoc Company, Inc.

The hydraulic/mechanical steering gear and rudder shaft on the ADAM E. CORNELIUS June 6, 1959.

Wisconsin Maritime Museum & The Manitowoc Company, Inc.
The boiler control panel on the ADAM E. CORNELIUS June 6, 1959.

Wisconsin Maritime Museum & The Manitowoc Company, Inc.
Stokers on the ADAM E. CORNELIUS June 6, 1959.

Chapter 5: ADAM E. CORNELIUS III 275

Wisconsin Maritime Museum & The Manitowoc Company, Inc.

Self-unloading conveyer and elevator drive machinery on the ADAM E. CORNELIUS June 6, 1959.

Wisconsin Maritime Museum & The Manitowoc Company, Inc.

One of the tunnels is shown on the ADAM E. CORNELIUS June 6, 1959.

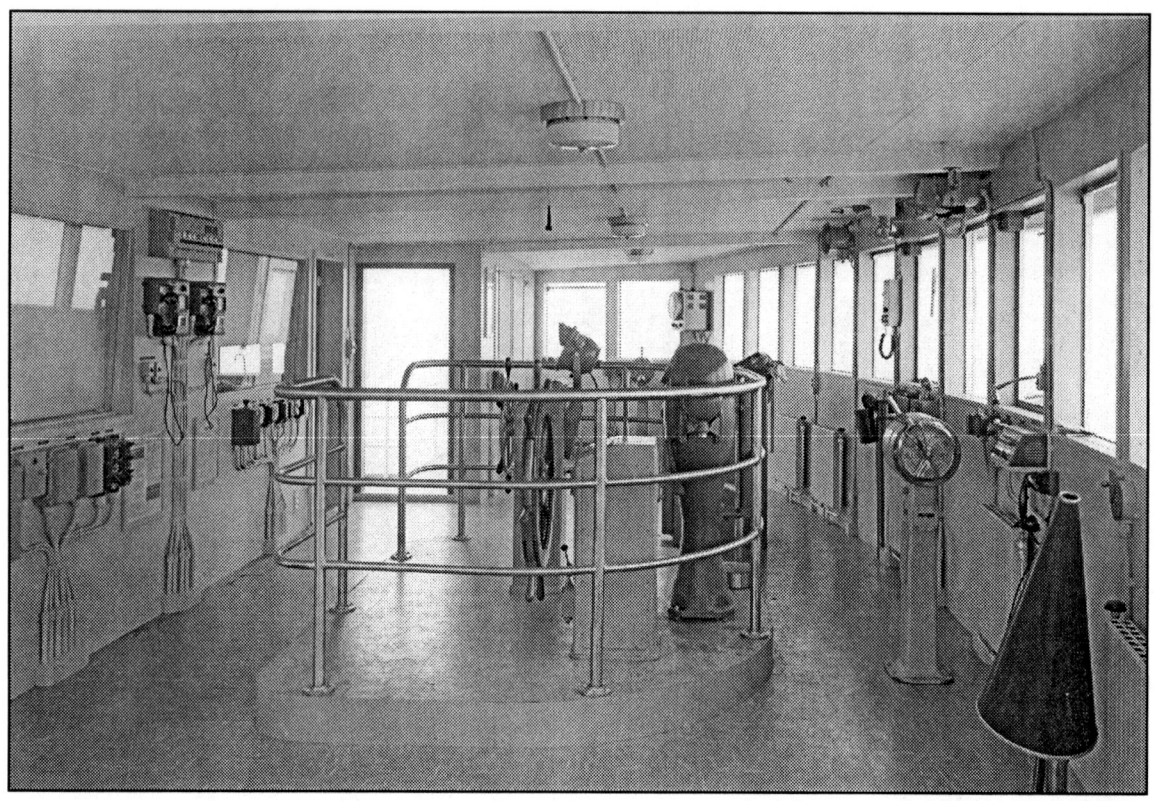

Wisconsin Maritime Museum & The Manitowoc Company, Inc.

The helm in the pilot house is shown looking to port on the ADAM E. CORNELIUS June 6, 1959.

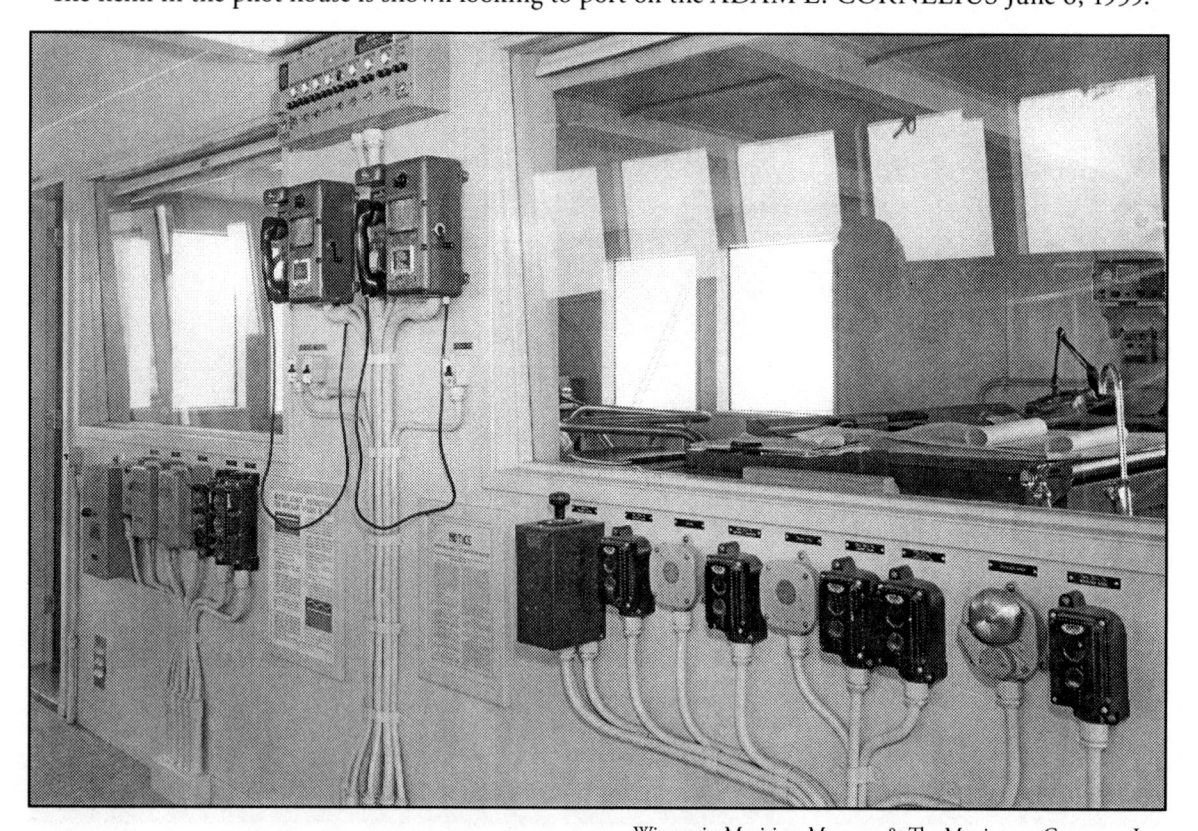

Wisconsin Maritime Museum & The Manitowoc Company, Inc.

View looking aft from the pilot house into the navigation room
of the ADAM E. CORNELIUS June 6, 1959.

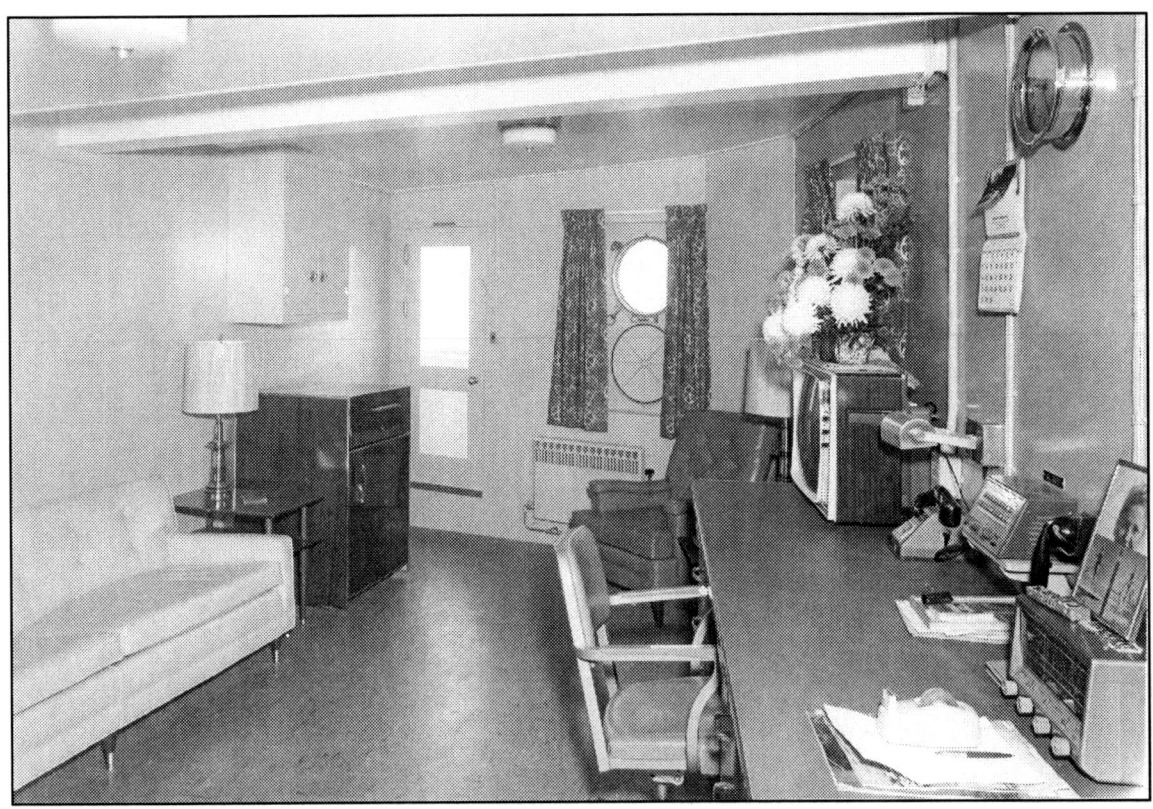

Wisconsin Maritime Museum & The Manitowoc Company, Inc.

The captain's office on the ADAM E. CORNELIUS June 6, 1959.

Wisconsin Maritime Museum & The Manitowoc Company, Inc.

The captain's quarters on the ADAM E. CORNELIUS June 6, 1959.

Wisconsin Maritime Museum & The Manitowoc Company, Inc.

Crew's dining room on the ADAM E. CORNELIUS June 6, 1959.

Wisconsin Maritime Museum & The Manitowoc Company, Inc.

Officers' dining room on the ADAM E. CORNELIUS June 6, 1959.

Chapter 5: ADAM E. CORNELIUS III

Wisconsin Maritime Museum & The Manitowoc Company, Inc.

View of the aft deck house with hatch covers in the foreground and downtown Manitowoc in the background from the ADAM E. CORNELIUS June 6, 1959.

Wisconsin Maritime Museum & The Manitowoc Company, Inc.

The self-unloading boom and hatch covers are shown in the foreground with the self-unloading boom support frame, elevator, and pilot house in the background on the ADAM E. CORNELIUS June 6, 1959.

Wisconsin Maritime Museum & The Manitowoc Company, Inc.
The self-unloading elevator and conveyer shoot of the Adam E. CORNELIUS June 6, 1959.

Wisconsin Maritime Museum & The Manitowoc Company, Inc.
View looking aft from outside of the pilot house over the self-unloading elevator
and boom support frame of the ADAM E. CORNELIUS June 6, 1959.

Wisconsin Maritime Museum & The Manitowoc Company, Inc.

The aft anchor windlass and a spare propeller blade in the lower right
are shown on the ADAM E. CORNELIUS June 6, 1959.

Wisconsin Maritime Museum & The Manitowoc Company, Inc.

View aft over the ADAM E. CORNELIUS with key Manitowoc landmarks in the background
including the Rahr Malting Grain Elevator, the Eighth Street Bridge, the Northern Grain Elevator
and between the self-unloading frames, the Manitowoc County Courthouse June 6, 1959.

CHAPTER 6

EDWARD L. RYERSON

<u>EDWARD L. RYERSON 1960 Hull # 425</u>   <u>Official No. 282106</u>

    Mr. Edward Larned Ryerson came from a family long involved in the iron and steel business. He was born in Chicago, Illinois on December 3, 1886 and graduated from Yale University with a PhD. degree in 1908. Mr. Ryerson started his career in the family business in Chicago in 1909. He was president of Joseph T. Ryerson & Son, Inc. when it was merged into Inland Steel in 1935. He served as chairman of Inland and Ryerson from 1940 to 1953. In 1958, Mr. Ryerson was chief of the delegation of American steel and ore mining representatives to the U. S. S. R., as well as director or trustee on many public service councils and commissions around Chicago. The steamer EDWARD L. RYERSON honors the man who was vice chairman of the board of both Inland Steel Company and his own company. Mr. Ryerson died August 2, 1971.

    <u>Manitowoc Shipbuilding, Inc., Manitowoc, Wisconsin</u>
- Customer – Inland Steel Company
- Designer – H. C. Downer and Associates
- Plans and specifications – Steel bulk carrier – length 730 feet – length between perpendiculars 712 feet – length of keel 702 feet – beam 75 feet – depth 39 feet – draft 26 feet 6 inches – gross tons 12,170 – net tons 7,637 – displacement 34,135 long tons – light ship weight 8,080 long tons – deadweight 26,055 long tons – forward boom length 250 feet – hatches, 18 on 24 foot centers, 54 feet wide X 20 feet long – 4 cargo holds – ballast tanks 17 – service speed 16.75 miles per hour – total crew 37 plus 8 guests – cost $8,000,000 – 30 miles of marine wire – 6 miles of piping – 200 miles of weld – 10,500 gallons of paint
- Engine – General Electric steam cross compound turbine – General Electric double reduction gear – 9,900 horsepower maximum – 9,000 horsepower normal at 9556 high pressure turbine revolutions per minute and 4156 low pressure turbine revolutions per minute and 105 propeller shaft revolutions per minute
- Boilers – Two Combustion Engineering, Inc. – two drum – bent tube – 465 pounds per square inch gauge at 765 degrees F
- Fuel – oil – capacity 214,900 gallons or 770 long tons
- Propeller – 20 feet diameter X 14 feet pitch – 5 blade – stainless steel – 6686 pounds
- Propeller shaft – diameter 21.63 inches – length 40 feet tailshaft plus three 16 foot 4 inch line shafts
- Generators – Two Westinghouse steam turbine – 600 kilowatts
- Construction
  - Keel laid – April 20, 1959
  - Launch – January 21, 1960
  - Sea trials – August 1, 1960
  - Commissioned – August 4, 1960
  - Delivered – August 4, 1960
- Average cargo – 23,500 tons

Maximum cargo – 26,930 tons

Log – The EDWARD L. RYERSON sailed August 4, 1960 from Manitowoc, Wisconsin to Escanaba, Michigan to load iron ore for Indiana Harbor, Indiana on its maiden voyage. The steamer set a new peak iron ore cargo record of 23, 378 tons in 1961 and again on August 28, 1962 at the Great Northern Railway's Allouez docks in Superior, Wisconsin when it took on 25,018 tons for Indiana Harbor. This record held for iron ore loaded well into 1965.

Bow thruster 1969

Laid up/museum Sturgeon Bay, Wisconsin 1998 – 2006

Current status – in service for Mittal Steel

Wisconsin Maritime Museum & The Manitowoc Company, Inc.

Celebrating the keel laying of the EDWARD L. RYERSON on April, 20 1959, left to right are Robert D. West, J. E. Theill, W. L. Wallace, Carl Jacobs, Edward L. Ryerson, Carl Tripp, Riley O'Brien, L. J. Sundlie, John D. West and Arthur Zuehlke.

Chapter 6: EDWARD L. RYERSON

Wisconsin Maritime Museum & The Manitowoc Company, Inc.

More bottom plates are in place on the keel blocks with many prefabricated double bottom sections in the background for the EDWARD L. RYERSON May 1, 1959.

Wisconsin Maritime Museum & The Manitowoc Company, Inc.

More bottom plates with the first double bottom section in place on the EDWARD L. RYERSON May 15, 1959.

Wisconsin Maritime Museum & The Manitowoc Company, Inc.

Full width bottom plates with more double bottom sections are in place on the EDWARD L. RYERSON June 1, 1959.

Wisconsin Maritime Museum & The Manitowoc Company, Inc.

The first double bottom side sections are in place with two Speedcranes on the double bottom of the EDWARD L. RYERSON June 15, 1959.

Wisconsin Maritime Museum & The Manitowoc Company, Inc.

Bow view of the double bottom side sections of the EDWARD L. RYERSON June 15, 1959.

Wisconsin Maritime Museum & The Manitowoc Company, Inc.

The bottom plates are tapering toward the stern with more double bottom and side sections in place on the EDWARD L. RYERSON June 15, 1959.

Wisconsin Maritime Museum & The Manitowoc Company, Inc.

A double bottom and side section is being placed on the port
side of the EDWARD L. RYERSON July 1, 1959.

Wisconsin Maritime Museum & The Manitowoc Company, Inc.

Hoisting an upper side section into place with the double bottom plates starting to taper toward the bow of
the EDWARD L. RYERSON July 1, 1959. Note the first deck beams are in place in the center background.

Chapter 6: EDWARD L. RYERSON 289

Wisconsin Maritime Museum & The Manitowoc Company, Inc.

Bottom plates are tapering toward the stern of the EDWARD L. RYERSON with a
double bottom section laying on top of the aft double bottom July 7, 1959.

Wisconsin Maritime Museum & The Manitowoc Company, Inc.

View from across the Manitowoc River of the EDWARD L. RYERSON also showing many
of the prefabrication buildings of the Manitowoc Shipbuilding Company July 7, 1959.

Wisconsin Maritime Museum & The Manitowoc Company, Inc.

Stern view from across the Manitowoc River of the EDWARD L. RYERSON also showing many of the prefabrication buildings of the Manitowoc Shipbuilding Company July 7, 1959.

Wisconsin Maritime Museum & The Manitowoc Company, Inc.

View from across the Manitowoc River of the EDWARD L. RYERSON August 1, 1959. Note that there are five cranes working on the EDWARD L. RYERSON.

Chapter 6: EDWARD L. RYERSON

Wisconsin Maritime Museum & The Manitowoc Company, Inc.

Double bottom stern sections being welded in place with more upper side sections
and deck beams in place on the EDWARD L. RYERSON August 1, 1959.

Wisconsin Maritime Museum & The Manitowoc Company, Inc.

The EDWARD L. RYERSON with bow double bottom pieces in place
and still covered with scaffolding on August 16, 1959.

Wisconsin Maritime Museum & The Manitowoc Company, Inc.

Work on the propeller shaft bearing, rudder stock and fairing casting of the EDWARD L. RYERSON with many prefabricated pieces in the background August 16, 1959.

Wisconsin Maritime Museum & The Manitowoc Company, Inc.

The still fully scaffold covered EDWARD L. RYERSON with bow side sections in place September 1, 1959.

Chapter 6: EDWARD L. RYERSON

Wisconsin Maritime Museum & The Manitowoc Company, Inc.

Hoisting the last double bottom piece into place on the stern with more sides completed on the EDWARD L. RYERSON September 1, 1959.

Wisconsin Maritime Museum & The Manitowoc Company, Inc.

The first upper stern section is being hoisted into place on the EDWARD L. RYERSON September 15, 1959.

The completed propeller shaft bearing, rudder stock and fairing casting is in position on the last keel blocks of the EDWARD L. RYERSON September 15, 1959.

Chapter 6: EDWARD L. RYERSON 295

Wisconsin Maritime Museum & The Manitowoc Company, Inc.

Side sections and double bottom sections are starting to form the
bow of the EDWARD L. RYERSON October 2, 1959.

Wisconsin Maritime Museum & The Manitowoc Company, Inc.

Numerous sections and decks have been added to the stern of
the EDWARD L. RYERSON October 2, 1959.

Wisconsin Maritime Museum & The Manitowoc Company, Inc.
The first view of the completed midsection of the EDWARD L. RYERSON October 2, 1959.

Wisconsin Maritime Museum & The Manitowoc Company, Inc.
More completed midsection with bow framing in progress on the
left, of EDWARD L. RYERSON October 15, 1959.

Wisconsin Maritime Museum & The Manitowoc Company, Inc.

View from the water of stern upper frame construction on the
EDWARD L. RYERSON November 2, 1959.

Wisconsin Maritime Museum & The Manitowoc Company, Inc.

Yard side view of stern construction on the EDWARD L. RYERSON, with frames adjoining the propeller shaft bearing, rudder stock and fairing casting in the lower left on November 2, 1959.

Wisconsin Maritime Museum & The Manitowoc Company, Inc.

Bow construction on the EDWARD L. RYERSON November 16, 1959, showing the forward bulkhead and lower bow frames.

Wisconsin Maritime Museum & The Manitowoc Company, Inc.

View from across the Manitowoc River showing upper stern construction and the completed mid body of the EDWARD L. RYERSON November 16, 1959.

Wisconsin Maritime Museum & The Manitowoc Company, Inc.

With the bow and stern taking shape on the completed mid body, it can be seen that the EDWARD L. RYERSON covered all of the yard's straight line frontage on December 2, 1959.

Wisconsin Maritime Museum & The Manitowoc Company, Inc.

More bow construction showing the forepeak in place on the
EDWARD L. RYERSON December 17, 1959.

Wisconsin Maritime Museum & The Manitowoc Company, Inc.

Stern view from across the river of the EDWARD L. RYERSON showing stern construction and the first aft deck house piece December 17, 1959.

Wisconsin Maritime Museum & The Manitowoc Company, Inc.

Stern view shows the nearly completed hull of the EDWARD L. RYERSON January 6, 1960. Note the heavy ice in the river.

Chapter 6: EDWARD L. RYERSON 301

Wisconsin Maritime Museum & The Manitowoc Company, Inc.

The bow of the EDWARD L. RYERSON is nearing completion on January 14, 1960.

Wisconsin Maritime Museum & The Manitowoc Company, Inc.

The launch trigger mechanism with a heavily greased skid in the foreground
under the bow of the EDWARD L. RYERSON January 20, 1960.

Wisconsin Maritime Museum & The Manitowoc Company, Inc.

Stern bunks and more greased skids under the EDWARD L. RYERSON with a good view of the propeller hub and rudder January 20, 1960.

Wisconsin Maritime Museum & The Manitowoc Company, Inc.

Near launch time showing the enclosed launch party stand for the EDWARD L. RYERSON January 21, 1960.

Chapter 6: EDWARD L. RYERSON 303

Wisconsin Maritime Museum, Daryl Cornick & The Manitowoc Company, Inc.
View of the launch of the EDWARD L. RYERSON from the yard January 21, 1960.

Wisconsin Maritime Museum, Daryl Cornick & The Manitowoc Company, Inc.
Bow and side view of the launch of the EDWARD L. RYERSON
into the Manitowoc River January 21, 1960.

Foredeck construction on the EDWARD L. RYERSON February 2, 1960.

Aft deck house construction on the EDWARD L. RYERSON February 2, 1960.

Wisconsin Maritime Museum & The Manitowoc Company, Inc.

Upper foredeck and forward deck house construction on the EDWARD L. RYERSON February 15, 1960.

Wisconsin Maritime Museum & The Manitowoc Company, Inc.

View from across the Manitowoc River of the aft deck house under construction on the EDWARD L. RYERSON February 15, 1960.

Wisconsin Maritime Museum, Daryl Cornick & The Manitowoc Company, Inc.

The forward deck house and pilot house in place with finish work in progress on the EDWARD L. RYERSON March 4, 1960.

Wisconsin Maritime Museum & The Manitowoc Company, Inc.

The aft deck house is under construction with the deck hatch crane in place on the EDWARD L. RYERSON April 16, 1960.

Wisconsin Maritime Museum & The Manitowoc Company, Inc.

Prefabricated aluminum hatch covers in the yard of the Manitowoc Shipbuilding Company awaiting installation on the EDWARD L. RYERSON May 10, 1960.

Wisconsin Maritime Museum & The Manitowoc Company, Inc.

Hatch covers are being installed on the deck of the EDWARD L. RYERSON with a view of the hatch crane May 10, 1960.

Wisconsin Maritime Museum, Daryl Cornick & The Manitowoc Company, Inc.

View from across the river of the bow of the EDWARD L. RYERSON with the state of the art styled forward mast in place May 14, 1960.

Wisconsin Maritime Museum, Daryl Cornick & The Manitowoc Company, Inc.

View from across the Manitowoc River on a calm morning showing more aft deck construction and the propeller blades installed on the EDWARD L. RYERSON May 14, 1960.

Chapter 6: EDWARD L. RYERSON

Wisconsin Maritime Museum, Daryl Cornick & The Manitowoc Company, Inc.

The streamlined stack being readied to hoist onto the EDWARD L. RYERSON May 23, 1960. Another innovation in ship design at the time was that the stack was fabricated of shiny stainless steel.

Wisconsin Maritime Museum, Daryl Cornick & The Manitowoc Company, Inc.

The stack is being hoisted onto the EDWARD L. RYERSON May 23, 1960. The actual exhaust pipes can be seen projecting up out of the aft deck house.

Wisconsin Maritime Museum, Daryl Cornick & The Manitowoc Company, Inc.

The stack is being lowered onto the EDWARD L. RYERSON May 13, 1960.

Wisconsin Maritime Museum, Daryl Cornick & The Manitowoc Company, Inc.

The EDWARD L. RYERSON is being painted showing the owning company's name on the side June 2, 1960. Note the navigation equipment is now on top the pilot house.

Wisconsin Maritime Museum, Daryl Cornick & The Manitowoc Company, Inc.

With the stylish stainless steel aft mast in place, the EDWARD L. RYERSON is nearly complete June 16, 1960.

Chapter 6: EDWARD L. RYERSON 313

Wisconsin Maritime Museum, Daryl Cornick & The Manitowoc Company, Inc.

Arial view of the EDWARD L. RYERSON half way through the Sooline or Jacknife bridge July 25, 1960.

Wisconsin Maritime Museum, Daryl Cornick & The Manitowoc Company, Inc.

End view showing the size of the EDWARD L. RYERSON
compared to the opening in the bridge July 25, 1960.

Wisconsin Maritime Museum, Daryl Cornick & The Manitowoc Company, Inc.

Arial view showing the bow of the EDWARD L. RYERSON approaching the shore line
that was dug out 30 feet for about 300 feet to clear the vessel's passage July 25, 1960.

Wisconsin Maritime Museum, Daryl Cornick & The Manitowoc Company, Inc.

The EDWARD L. RYERSON squeezed between the jackknife
bridge and the dug out shoreline July 25, 1960.

Chapter 6: EDWARD L. RYERSON 315

Wisconsin Maritime Museum, Daryl Cornick & The Manitowoc Company, Inc.

The bow of the EDWARD L. RYERSON pushed tight into the corner of the dug out area
and the stern just missing the shore on port and the bridge at the stern July 25, 1960.

Wisconsin Maritime Museum, Daryl Cornick & The Manitowoc Company, Inc.

With the stern clear of the bridge, the EDWARD L. RYERSON is now ready to back
up to clear the bow and proceed down the Manitowoc River July 25, 1960.

Wisconsin Maritime Museum, Daryl Cornick & The Manitowoc Company, Inc.

View looking aft from the pilot house over the deck hatches and aft deck house with the Manitowoc Harbor in the background August 1, 1960.

Wisconsin Maritime Museum, Daryl Cornick & The Manitowoc Company, Inc.

The deck hatch crane is shown on the EDWARD L. RYERSON August 1, 1960.

Wisconsin Maritime Museum, Daryl Cornick & The Manitowoc Company, Inc.

A spectacular view from on top of the EDWARD L. RYERSON pilot house shows the foremast looking aft at the aft mast August 1, 1960. Navigation equipment shown from left to right include radio telephone antenna, radar antenna, port and starboard navigation lights, anemometer, wind vane and to the far right is the radio direction finder antenna.

Wisconsin Maritime Museum, Daryl Cornick & The Manitowoc Company, Inc.

The aft deck house with the stylish yet functional aft mast and stack with deck lights, horns, and loading level lights on the EDWARD L. RYERSON August 1, 1960.

Chapter 6: EDWARD L. RYERSON 319

Wisconsin Maritime Museum, Daryl Cornick & The Manitowoc Company, Inc.
Bow anchor windlass on the EDWARD L. RYERSON August 1, 1960.

Wisconsin Maritime Museum, Daryl Cornick & The Manitowoc Company, Inc.
View looking to starboard of the pilot house on the EDWARD L. RYERSON August 1, 1960.

Wisconsin Maritime Museum, Daryl Cornick & The Manitowoc Company, Inc.
Chart room of the EDWARD L. RYERSON August 1, 1960.

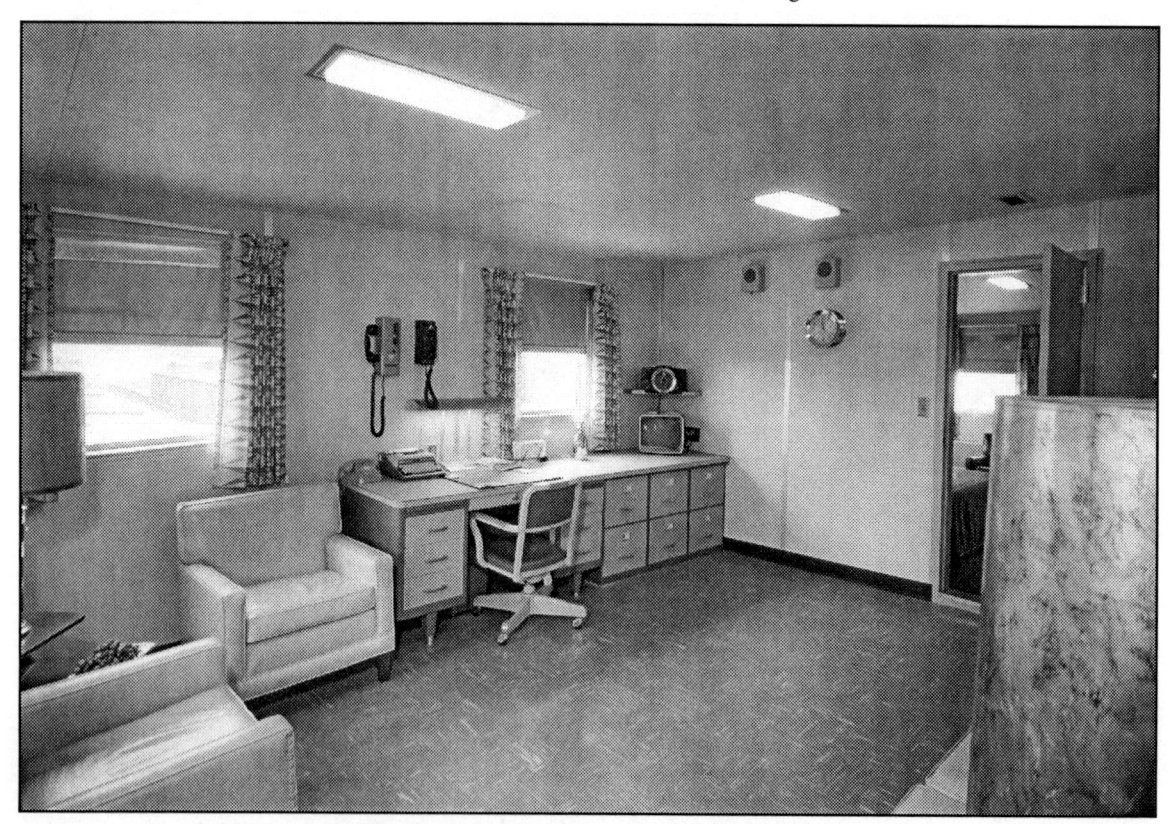

Wisconsin Maritime Museum, Daryl Cornick & The Manitowoc Company, Inc.
The captain's office on the EDWARD L. RYERSON August 1, 1960.

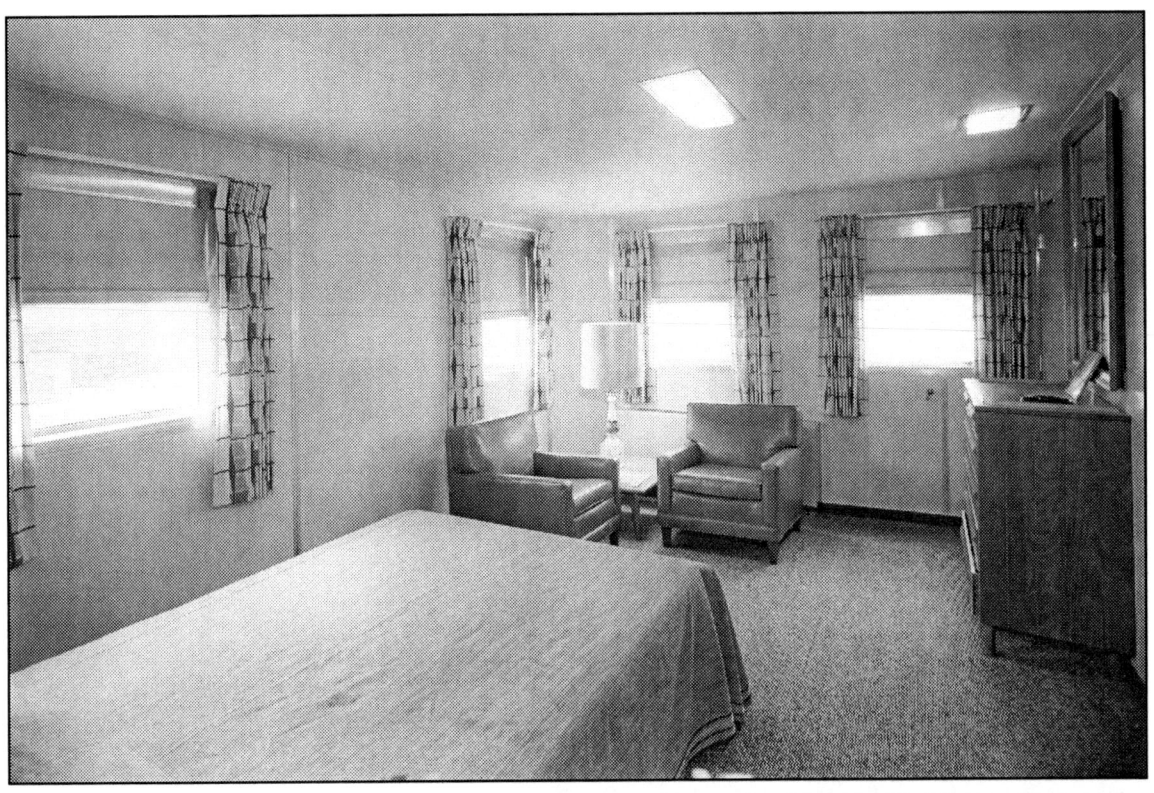

Wisconsin Maritime Museum, Daryl Cornick & The Manitowoc Company, Inc.
The captain's quarters on the EDWARD L. RYERSON August 1, 1960.

Wisconsin Maritime Museum, Daryl Cornick & The Manitowoc Company, Inc.
The guests' dining room on the EDWARD L. RYERSON August 1, 1960.

Wisconsin Maritime Museum, Daryl Cornick & The Manitowoc Company, Inc.
The officers' dining room on the EDWARD L. RYERSON August 1, 1960.

Wisconsin Maritime Museum, Daryl Cornick & The Manitowoc Company, Inc.
The crew's dining room is in the aft deck house on the EDWARD L. RYERSON August 1, 1960.

Chapter 6: EDWARD L. RYERSON

Wisconsin Maritime Museum, Daryl Cornick & The Manitowoc Company, Inc.
The galley on the EDWARD L. RYERSON features every convenience
of the time all in stainless steel August 1, 1960.

Wisconsin Maritime Museum, Daryl Cornick & The Manitowoc Company, Inc.
The guests' lounge has an aft view from the forward deck house
on the EDWARD L. RYERSON August 1, 1960.

Wisconsin Maritime Museum, Daryl Cornick & The Manitowoc Company, Inc.
Here is another view of the guests' lounge on the EDWARD L. RYERSON August 1, 1960.

Wisconsin Maritime Museum, Daryl Cornick & The Manitowoc Company, Inc.
The engine control console on the EDWARD L. RYERSON August 1, 1960.

Chapter 6: EDWARD L. RYERSON 325

Wisconsin Maritime Museum, Daryl Cornick & The Manitowoc Company, Inc.
View of the engine room on the EDWARD L. RYERSON August 1, 1960.

Wisconsin Maritime Museum, Daryl Cornick & The Manitowoc Company, Inc.
The high pressure General Electric steam turbine is shown to the left with the top of the low pressure turbine in the foreground on the EDWARD L. RYERSON August 1, 1960.

Wisconsin Maritime Museum, Daryl Cornick & The Manitowoc Company, Inc.

Another view shows the engine control panel on the right with the electrical controls on the left on the EDWARD L. RYERSON August 1, 1960.

Wisconsin Maritime Museum, Daryl Cornick & The Manitowoc Company, Inc.

Boiler controls on the EDWARD L. RYERSON August 1, 1960.

Wisconsin Maritime Museum, Daryl Cornick & The Manitowoc Company, Inc.

The electrical control panel on the EDWARD L. RYERSON August 1, 1960.

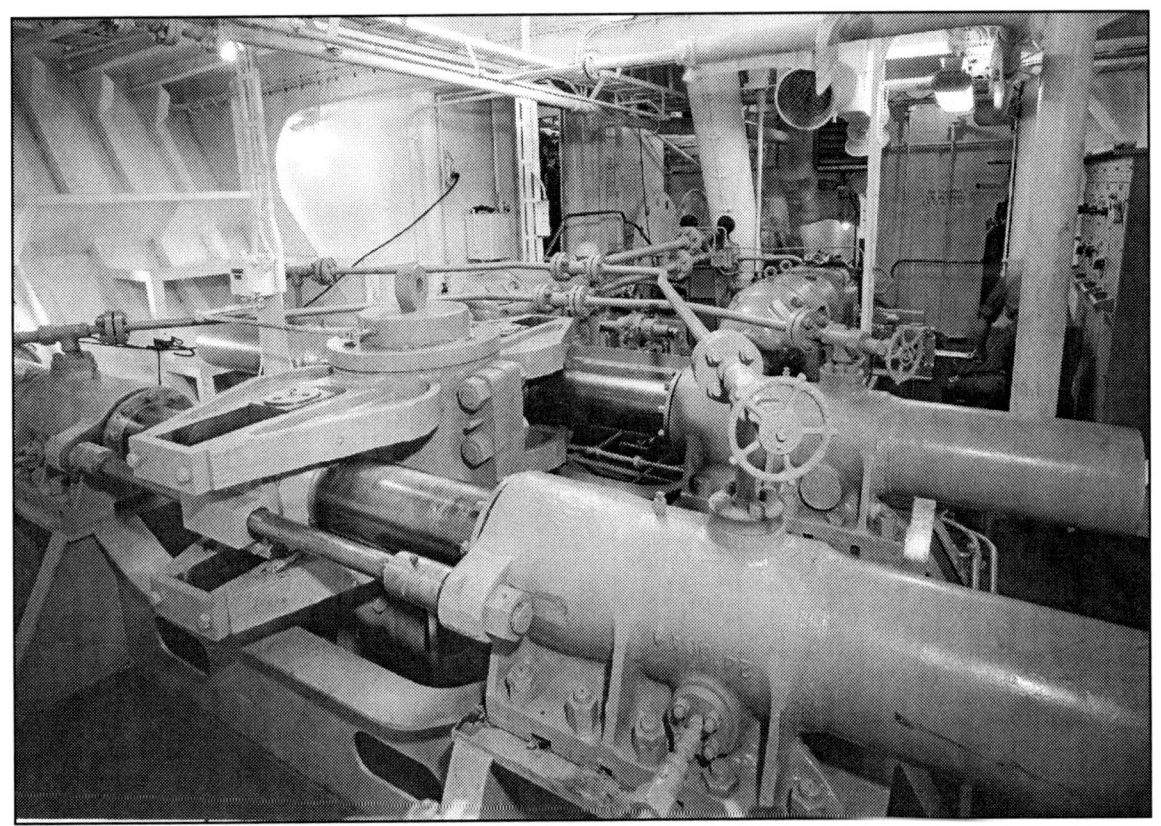

Wisconsin Maritime Museum, Daryl Cornick & The Manitowoc Company, Inc.

The electro/hydraulic/mechanical steering gear and rudder shaft
on the EDWARD L. RYERSON August 1, 1960.

Wisconsin Maritime Museum, Daryl Cornick & The Manitowoc Company, Inc.

It is a long walk through one of the tunnels of the EDWARD L. RYERSON August 1, 1960.

Wisconsin Maritime Museum, Daryl Cornick & The Manitowoc Company, Inc.

The propeller shaft and bearings of the EDWARD L. RYERSON August 1, 1960.

Chapter 6: EDWARD L. RYERSON 329

Wisconsin Maritime Museum, Daryl Cornick & The Manitowoc Company, Inc.
The stainless steel propeller and rudder of the EDWARD L. RYERSON August 1, 1960.

Wisconsin Maritime Museum, Daryl Cornick & The Manitowoc Company, Inc.

View of the stern of the EDWARD L. RYERSON on sea trials in Lake Michigan August 1, 1960. Note that ballast was added in the stern tanks to submerge the propeller.

Wisconsin Maritime Museum, Daryl Cornick & The Manitowoc Company, Inc.

The EDWARD L. RYERSON with the City of Manitowoc in the distant background August 1, 1960.

Chapter 6: EDWARD L. RYERSON 331

Wisconsin Maritime Museum, Daryl Cornick & The Manitowoc Company, Inc.
Another view of the EDWARD L. RYERSON on sea trials in Lake Michigan August 1, 1960.

Wisconsin Maritime Museum, Daryl Cornick & The Manitowoc Company, Inc.
Aft quarter view of the EDWARD L. RYERSON on sea trials August 1, 1960.

Wisconsin Maritime Museum, Daryl Cornick & The Manitowoc Company, Inc.

Parting shot August 4, 1960.

Epilogue

1968 Arthur J. Zuehlke became president.

With the difficulty of getting the EDWARD L. RYERSON out of the Manitowoc River, it was evident that 730 feet long by 75 feet wide was the largest vessel that could be delivered out of the Manitowoc Shipbuilding Company yard. During the years 1962 through 1968 the Poe Lock was built at Sault Ste. Marie, Michigan. This lock was 1200 feet long by 110 feet wide by 32 feet deep. This opened the door to building vessels considerably larger than 730 feet by 75 feet. To build these anticipated larger vessels, Manitowoc Shipbuilding had to find a new location that had navigable water ways for larger vessels. Only 65 miles to the north was Sturgeon Bay, Wisconsin that had three shipyards, two of which had open bay waters navigable to Lake Michigan, capable of floating ships of any conceivable size. From 1968 through 1970, acquisitions were made and most of Manitowoc Shipbuilding equipment and personnel were moved to Sturgeon Bay and became Bay Shipbuilding Corp.

Manitowoc Shipbuilder Chronology

Captain Joseph V. Edwards	1847 to 1851
Bates and Son	1852 to 1861
Elias Sorenson	1852 to 1856
Rand and Harbridge	1853
Hanson Rand	1854 to 1856
Greenleaf S. Rand	1856 to 1873
Henry B. Burger	1867 to 1873
Jonah Richards	1867 to 1874
Jasper Hanson and E. W. Packard	1868
Jasper Hanson	1869 to 1871
E. W. Packard	1869
Peter Larson	1869 to 1881
Hanson and Scove	1871 to 1889
Mads Ornes	1872 to 1888
James Butler	1873 to 1883
Larson and Son	1873
Rand and Burger	1873 to 1884
Gunder Jorgenson	1875 to 1881
Captain Francis P. Williams	1882 to 1885
Burger and Burger	1886 to 1902
Manitowoc Dry Dock Company	1902 to 1910
Manitowoc Shipbuilding and Dry Dock Company	1910 to 1916
Manitowoc Shipbuilding Company	1916 to 1920
Manitowoc Shipbuilding Corporation	1916 to 1937
Manitowoc Shipbuilding Company	1937 to 1952
Manitowoc Shipbuilding, Inc.	1952 to 1968
Bay Shipbuilding Company	1968 to present

BIBLIOGRAPHY

Great Lakes Ships We Remember by Peter Van Der Linden

Frederickson's History of the Ann Arbor Auto And Train Ferries by Arthur C. and Lucy F. Frederickson

Pictorial History of the C & O Train and Auto Ferries and Pere Marquette Line Steamers by Arthur C. and Lucy F. Frederickson

Fresh Water Submarines The Manitowoc Story by Rear Admiral William T. Nelson U.S.N. (Ret.)

Manitowoc Submarines

Schooner Days In Door County by Walter M. and Mary K. Hirthe

Great Lakes Bulk Carriers 1869-1985 by John F. Devendorf

Marge Miley Milestones Manitowoc Herald Times

Red Stacks Over The Horizon the Story Of The Goodrich Steamboat Line James L. Elliott

Cargo Carriers Of The Great Lakes by Jacques Lesstrang

Ladies of the Lakes by Jim Clary

Steamboat Bill by Rev. F. C. St. Clair

Manitowoc Herald Times

Captain Edward Carus Scrapbook

Ships and Shipwrecks in Door County, Wisconsin by Arthur C. And Lucy F. Frederickson

Frederickson's Chart of Ships Wrecked in the Vicinity of Door County, Wisconsin

Namesakes Of The '90s by John O. Greenwood

Wild Gales and Tattered Sails by Paul J. Creviere, Jr.

Herman G. Runge Collection Milwaukee Public Library

Jonah Richards by Vickie Peaslee

Manitowoc County Historical Society

Norwegian Sailors on the Great Lakes by Knut Gjerset

Manitowoc Marine Group

Inland Seas Marine Museum

History of Manitowoc County by Ralph G. Plumb

Know Your Lakers of World War One by Rev. Edward J. Dowling

Great Lakes Bulk Ore Carrier Edward L. Ryerson by C. E. Tripp, G. F. Rankin, J. G. Souris, R. H. Miller

Lake Boats 2002 by John O. Greenwood and Michael J. Dills

Burger Family by Doris Burger Hansen

Voyage of Vision

James Butler and Hans Scove by Barbara Nitka

Bowling Green State University Historical Collections of the Great Lakes

Wooden Steamers on the Great Lakes by Rodney H. Mills

Merchant Vessels of the United States

Divers guide to Michigan by Steve Harrington

Index

A

A. A. CARPENTER 60–61
A. BAENSCH 15
A.B.C.F.M. 28
A. C. AMES 65
ACHING HEARTS 80
ADAM E. CORNELIUS II 125
ADAM E. CORNELIUS III 249–282
A. D. HAYWARD 71
ALABAMA 90–91
ALICE 62–63
ALICE RICHARDS 25
ANNIE THORINE 10
ANN ARBOR #6 125
ANN ARBOR #7 106–107
ARIZONA 78
ARTHUR K. ATKINSON 125

B

BARNES 24
Bates, Stephen 3
Bates, William W. 3, 25
Bates and Son 3, 9, 335
Bay Shipbuilding 113, 333, 335
BELLE 6
BLACKHAWK 5
BLAZING STAR 26
Burger, George B. 22, 70, 87, 91
Burger, Henry B. 22–23, 25, 26, 50, 70, 86, 335
Burger and Burger 33, 41, 58, 70, 76, 84, 86, 87, 335
BURT BARNES 63–64
Butler, James 25, 44, 45, 48, 335, 338

C

CANANOVA 102
CAPTAIN EDWARD V. SMITH 249
Case and Clark 1
CAYO MAMBI 102
C. C. BARNES 24–25
CHALLENGE 4, 5
CHARLES C. WEST 107
CHARLES LULING 34
CHEQUAMEGON 87–88
CHICAGO 51–53, 75
CHICAGO BOARD OF TRADE 16
CHRISTINA NILSSON 36
CITIZEN 2
CITY OF FLINT 32 111–112
CITY OF GREEN BAY 125
CITY OF LUDINGTON 58, 86
CITY OF MANITOWOC 25–26
CITY OF MARQUETTE 80
CITY OF MIDLAND 41 113
CITY OF MILWAUKEE 112
CITY OF RACINE 78
CITY OF SAGINAW 31 111
CITY OF WOODSTOCK 34
CLARA 63
CLIPPER CITY 5
C. L. JOHNSON 30
COLLIER 60
COLONEL GLOVER 5, 9
CONVOY 3
COPRES 97
COQUINA 97
CORAPEAK 97
CORA A. 77
CORCORAN 98
CORNELLIA B. WINDIATE 45
CORNUCOPIA 98
CORONA 19
CORRALES 96
CORSICANA 96
COTTON BLOSSOM 60

D

DAISY DAY 38
DANIEL MCCOOL 108–109
DAVID VANCE 46
DEPERE 50
DETROIT EDISON II 233–247
Dry dock 14, 25, 33, 43, 50, 54, 84, 91, 104, 106, 108, 114

E

Edwards, Captain Joseph V. 2, 6, 335
EDWARD BUCKLEY 83
EDWARD L. RYERSON 283–333
EDWIN S. TICE 71–72, 75
EL TEMPO 15
EMILY B. MAXWELL 40
EMMA L. NIELSEN 41
E. M. SHOYER 10
ESPINDOLA 31
EUGENE C. HART 82

F

FALMOUTH 37
FANNIE C. HART 76
FARRAND H. WILLIAMS 69
FELICITOUS 32–33
FLEETWING 23
FRANCIS HINTON 43

G

G. C. TRUMPF 44–45
Geer, Lynford E. 87, 88
GEORGE 22
GEORGE MURRAY 22
GEORGIA 58, 86
GESINE 12
GILBERT KNAPP 31–32
G. J. BOYCE 67
GLAD TIDINGS 48
GOLET 118
Goodrich, Albert E. 3, 14
GRACE WILLIAMS 69
GRAND RAPIDS 109
GREYHOUND 17
GUAVINA 119
GUIDO 11–12
GUIDO FPISTER 37–38
GUITARRO 119
Gunnell, Elias 86, 87, 103, 108
Gunnell Machine Company 88, 90
Gunnell Tool Company 88

H

HAMMERHEAD 119
Hanson, Jasper 25, 26, 27, 36, 335
Hanson and Scove 36, 49, 335
Hanson Rand 12, 13, 14, 335
HARDHEAD 119
HATTIE A. ESTELL 37
HAWKBILL 119
H. B. BURGER 55
H. C. ALBRECHT 28
H. E. MCALLISTER 30
HENRIETTA ESCH 46
HENRY C. RICHARDS 24
HENRY WHITBECK 59
H. M. SCOVE 38
H. RAND 14–15

I

ICEFISH 120
IMPERIAL 59–60
INDIANA 80–82
INDUSTRY 31
IOWA 21, 85
ISAAC WATSON STEPHENSON 57
ISABELLA J. BOYCE 78–79
ISOLDA BOCK 68

J

JALLAO 120
JAMES H. HALL 42
J. A. STORNACH 28
J. B. NEWLAND 28–29
J. C. PERRETT 65
J. DUVALL 54–55
JESSIE PHILLIPS 26
J. I. CASE 53–54
J. LOOMIS MC CLAREN 41
JOHN A. KLING 103–104
JOHN E. HALL 44
JOHN G. MUNSON 127–166, 170, 172, 174
JOHN J. BOLAND III 167–213
Jorgenson, Captain Gunder 49, 67, 335
JO VILAS 16
JULIA LARSON 34–35
J. V. JONES 55

K

KATE L. BRUCE 36
KETE 120
KRAKEN 121

L

LAGARTO 121
LAKE ANNETTE 95
LAKE GADSDEN 98
LAKE GAITHER 99
LAKE GALATA 99
LAKE GALEWOOD 99
LAKE GALIEN 99
LAKE GALISTEO 99
LAKE GREENWOOD 95
LAKE HARESTI 100–101
LAKE HORUS 101
LAKE HYAS 101
LAKE HYBLA 101
LAKE HYGEIA 102
LAKE HYPANIA 102
LAKE IKATAN 100
LAKE KYTTLE 96
LAKE LIDA 94
LAKE LINDEN 95
LAKE MOHAWK 93

LAKE MONROE 94
LAKE ONAWA 98
LAKE ONEIDA 93
LAKE ONTARIO 93
LAKE PEWAUKEE 94
LAKE SAVUS 99
LAKE SHAWANO 94
LAKE VIEW 94
LAKE WILSON 95
LAKE WINTHROP 95
LALLAH ROOKH 48
LAMPREY 121
Larson, Peter 31, 335
Larson and Son 50, 335
LEADALE 103
LILY E. 27
LINERLA 42, 49
LIZARDFISH 121
LIZZIE METZNER 73
L. J. CONWAY 50
LOGGERHEAD 121
LOMIRA 9
LOTTIE COOPER 56–57
LOTUS 83–84
LOUISA MCDONALD 27
LOUIS MEEKER 37
LUCIA A. SIMPSON 55–56
LYDIA 51

M

MACABI 122
MADISON 110
MANITOWOC 18, 51, 108
Manitowoc Company Inc. 125
Manitowoc Dry Dock Company 25, 86, 87, 90, 335
Manitowoc Harbor 1, 154, 316
Manitowoc Shipbuilder Chronology 335
Manitowoc Shipbuilding, Inc. 125, 127, 167, 215, 249, 283, 335
Manitowoc Shipbuilding and Dry Dock Co. 92, 335
Manitowoc Shipbuilding Company 80, 93, 96, 112, 114, 167, 215, 289, 290, 307, 333, 335
Manitowoc Shipbuilding Corporation 103, 105, 106, 335
Manitowoc Steam Boiler Works 89, 93
MAPIRO 123
MARGARET A. MUIR 37
MARK B. COVELL 75–76
MARY C. PLATT 5
MARY L. HIGGIE 37
MARY STOCKTON 4
MAYWOOD 88–89
MAY RICHARDS 46–47

MELITTA 39
MENHADEN 123
MENOMINEE 21, 85
MERCHANT 35–36
MERO 123
MINNEHAHA 49
MISHICOTT 49
MOCKING BIRD 26
MUELLER 71
MUSKEGON 20–21
MYRTLE CAMP 83
MYSTIC STAR 44

N

NABOB 16
NAVARINO 20, 21
NEEDLEFISH 124
NERKA 124
NEVADA 92
NORLAND 82
NORTHWEST 17–18
NORTH STAR 11
NORTH YUBA 5

O

OCONTO 22
OLGA 61
ORION 17, 20
Ornes, Mads 42, 48, 335

P

Packard, E. W. 26, 30, 335
PENOBSCOT 57–58
PERE MARQUETTE #6 75
PERE MARQUETTE #7 87
PERE MARQUETTE 10 124
PERE MARQUETTE 12 110
PERE MARQUETTE 21 105–106
PERE MARQUETTE 22 106
PERE MARQUETTE 41 113
PETER REISS 125
PETO vii, 114–115
PETOSKY 73–74
POGY 115
POMPON 115
Prindeville, Thomas J. 87
PUFFER 116
PYTHON 98

R

RABALO 117

RAND 70
Rand, E. H. 13
Rand, E. K. 13, 16
Rand, Greenleaf S. 3, 14, 16, 25, 50, 67, 70, 335
Rand, Hanson 12, 13, 14, 335
Rand and Burger 50, 70, 335
Rand and Harbridge 12, 335
R. A. SEYMOUR JR. 65–66
RASHER 116
RATON 116
RAY 117
REDFIN 117
Richards, Jonah ix, 8, 14, 24, 25, 46, 47, 50, 335, 337
RIPON 100
R. KANTERS 34
ROANOKE 111
ROCK 118
ROGDAY 92
ROWE 76
RUBE RICHARDS 47

S

SAGINAW 168
SARAH SPENCER 249
S. A. WOOD 24
Scove, Hans M. ix, 36, 338
SEA BARGE ONE 249
SEA GEM 8
SHEBOYGAN 18–19, 75, 85
SHOW BOAT SAM 60
SIDNEY O. NEFF 80
SIOUX CITY 100
S. M. STEPHENSON 59
Sorenson, Elias 5, 9, 335
SOWARDS 70
STATE OF MICHIGAN 50
STEPHEN BATES 6
SUCCESS 67
SUNBEAM 7–8

T

TALLAHASSEE 36
TENNIE AND LAURA 67–68
THISTEL 50
THOMAS H. HOWLAND 37
THOMAS H. SMITH 61–62
THOMAS HUME 28
THOMAS L. PARKER 41
TOLEDO 9
TRANSIT 13
TRANSPORT 24
TRIAL 15

U

UNION 7
UNITED STATES 89

V

VICTOR 7
VIKING 106

W

WABASH 125
WAUKESHA 16, 17
WAUWATOSA 100
W. C. KIMBALL 49
West, Charles C. 86, 87, 103, 248
West, John D. 248, 284
WILLE KELLER 30
Williams, Captain Francis P. 69, 335
WILLIAM A. REISS 125
WILLIAM M. JONES 12
WILLIS 32
W. O. GOODMAN 66

Z

Zuehlke, Arthur J. 284, 333
Z.Y.M.C.A. 30

ABOUT THE AUTHOR

Tom Wenstadt was born and raised in Manitowoc, Wisconsin graduating from Lincoln High School. He has been interested in and has studied boats and ships all of his life. As a grade schooler, he watched intently as the last three freighters took shape. He remembers saying "Mom, remember to pick me up to see the launch!" Schools were always let out to watch a launch. His neighbors and friend's parents worked at the shipyard. He has been a Marine Engineer in the Great Lakes area for 30 years, with a Bachelors Degree in Mechanical Engineering from Michigan Technological University. His hobbies are Great Lakes shipping, boating and automobiles. His museum and historical society affiliations are: the Wisconsin Maritime Museum 1988, Wisconsin Marine Historical Society 2003, Door County Maritime Museum & Lighthouse Preservation Society 2003, Inland Sea Maritime Museum 2002 and the Society of Naval Architects and Marine Engineers 1996.